Questioning the Boundary Issues of Internet Security

2

GU01034582

Charles A. Shoniregun

Ioannis P. Chochliouros
Blandine Laperche
Oleksandr Logvynovskiy
Anastasia Spiliopoulou-
          Chochliourou

e-Centre for
Infonomics

Questioning The Boundary Issues of Internet Security

Charles A. Shoniregun
Ioannis P. Chochliouros
Blandine Laperche
Oleksandr Logvynovskiy
Anastasia Spiliopoulou-Chochliourou

Trademarks

All terms mentioned in this book that are known to be trademarks or service marks have been appropriately capitalised. The publisher cannot attest to the accuracy of this information. Use of a term in this book should not be regarded as affecting the validity of any trademark or service mark.

Warning and Disclaimer

Every effort has been made to make this book as complete and as accurate as possible, but no warranty or fitness is implied. The information provided is on "as is" basis. The authors and the publisher shall have neither liability nor responsibility to any person or entity with respect to any loss or damages arising from the information contained in this book.

ISBN: 0-9546628-0-6

First Printing: February 2004, Collegium Printers

Copyright © 2004 by e-Centre for Infonomics

Executive Editor:
Charles A. Shoniregun
Design:
Oleksandr Logvynovskiy

Contents

1

Electronic Commerce Mediations:
The Shape of Things to Come! 15

2

3

4

4.

Patentability: Questions About the Control of Strategic Technology 117

5

Next Generation Networks and Services: Regulation vs. Self-Regulation/Co-Regulation 141

6.*

List of Figures

List of Tables

About Authors

Charles Adetokunbo SHONIREGUN, has taught in many universities and colleges in the UK and abroad. He is a member of the research committee at the School of Computing and Technology and an elected member of the University of East London Academic Board. He has degrees from the University of East London, and a professional member of the British Computer Society (MBCS), Chartered Engineer (CEng), Information Risk Management and Audit (IRMA), Association for Computing Machinery (ACM), IEEE, IEEE Task Force on E-commerce, IEEE Technical Committee, Fellow of the Institution of Analysts and Programmers (FIAP) and a Fellow of the Royal Society for the encouragement of Arts, Manufacturers and Commerce (FRSA). He has also undertaken consultancy for various industrial sectors at the global platform and has over 15 years experience in the telecommunications industry. He is a guest speaker to many universities in the UK and abroad on issues relating to his research and consultancy area. His research interests are in the fields of Internet security, risks assessment of technology-enabled information, electronic and mobile commerce (emC), telecommunications and applied information systems. He is the Editor-in-Chief of the International Journal for Infonomics, an author, co-author, visiting and distinguished visiting professor in "Applied Internet Security and Information Systems", and External Assessor to many universities.

Ioannis P. CHOCHLIOUROS, is a Telecommunications Electrical Engineer, graduated from the Polytechnic School of the Aristotle University of Thessaloniki, Greece, holding also a MSc. & a Ph.D. from the University Pierre et Marie Curie, Paris VI, France. He worked as a Research and Teaching Assistant at the University Paris VI, in cooperation with other European countries. His practical experience as an engineer has been mainly in Telecommunications, as well as in various construction projects in Greece and the wider Balkan area. Since 1997 he has been working at the Competition Department and then as an engineer consultant of the Chief Technical Officer of OTE (Hellenic Telecoms S.A.), for regulatory and technical matters. He has been strongly involved in major OTE's national and international business activities, as a specialist consultant for technical and regulatory affairs. He currently works as the Head of Section for Technical Regulations of

Division for Standardization & Technical Regulations, and as a special Assistant to the Chief Officer for Technical Affairs of OTE's Group of Companies. He has been involved into different European and international projects and activities, while he has published various scientific and business papers & reports. He has also participated into many international Conferences, Workshops, Fora and other events, some of which as an invited speaker - official OTE's representative.

Blandine LAPERCHE, Assistant Professor –Economics Laboratoire Redéploiement Industriel et Innovation, Université du Littoral Dunkerque- France.

Oleksandr LOGVYNOVSKIY, is a Software Engineer, graduated from Kharkiv State University of Radioelectronics, Ukraine. He has published many research papers and currently a research candidate in computer science at the School Computing, Information Systems & Mathematics, London South Bank University. He is a member of the British Computer Society (BCS); Association of Developers and Users of Intelligent Systems (ADUIS), an affiliated society of European Coordinating Committee for Artificial Intelligence (ECCAI); and Network of Academics and Professionals (NAP), a section of European Distance Education Network (EDEN). His research and consultancy areas are in Semistructured Data Mining, electronic commerce (eC), intelligent agents, XML and Web-based Information Systems.

Anastasia SPILIOPOULOU-CHOCHLIOUROU, is a Lawyer, LLM, Member of the Athens Bar Association. Since 1992 she has gained extended experience as a lawyer, while she has been involved in various affairs. Her LLM's post-graduated degree, from the Athens University Law School, has been taken place with specific emphasis given to the investigation of the multiple regulatory aspects related to the Internet (infrastructure, services, software, content). During the latest years, she had a major participation in matters related to telecommunications & broadcasting policy, in Greece and abroad, within the framework of the Information Society. She has been involved in current research and business activities, as a specialist for E-Commerce, Electronic Signatures and other Information Society applications. She currently works as an OTE's (Hellenic Telecoms S.A.) lawyer-collaborator for the Division of Procurement and Services' Contracts of the Legal Department of OTE Group of Companies.

Dedication

Late Isaiah O. Shoniregun, Late Madam Alice O. Oyefeso
Late Madam Igbinyemi Shoniregun, Late Joseph K. Shoniregun,
Late sister Bisi and Late Bamidele Sosan

Charles A. Shoniregun

Acknowledgements

David Seth Preston (2001) mentioned in his book 'Technology, Managerialism and the University', how John Cleese hilariously, in receiving a dramatic award some years ago, produced an inordinately long list of acknowledgements. The list included his parents, around fifty philosophers and both his bookmaker and milkman. I now know how he felt but only brevity prevents me from imitating the great comic. However, I still have to say a big thank you to the following people:

Mike Thorne
Paul Smith
Roy Perryman
David Seth Preston
Sonny Nwankwo
Kazem Chaharbaghi
Chris Imafidon
Steve Martin
Jacquie Bolissian
Fadi Safieddine
Dolly Bridge
Joan Marshall
Vyacheslav Grebenyuk
Olga Kotukh
Jonathan Smith

Many thanks to all contributors and colleagues at the School of Computing and Technology (University of East London (UEL)), e-Centre for Infonomics and elsewhere who have provided useful comments on earlier drafts; in particular the comments of anonymous reviewers have been invaluable.

And tangential thanks go to my beauty queen and my angels.

Preface

'Questioning the Boundary Issues of Internet Security' brings together a convenient empirical research that has attempted to answer these questions. The chapters are chosen for their clarity, relevance, timeliness, and emphasises the connection of Internet technology with the world in which it is use. The human nature has led it self to the Internet, with the believe that whatever and however, can be reach without thinking of distance and time at minimum cost and high value for money, but the unlimited wants of our nature and technology advancements has been delimitation to Internet revolution.

However, it is not only just goods and services available to the consumer. Consumers can sell their own goods, either privately, on the auction web sites or through the 'free advert' papers than have gone on-line. With the convergence of transmission the Internet technology compresses and stores digitised information so that it can travel through existing phone, wireless and cable wiring systems. The communication systems that it provides transmission for are data, image and video over the same line. The convergence of transmission is advantageous for businesses and academicians as it is results in access to networks and in the creation of new, low-delivery channels for new and old products aimed at either existing customers or new customer segments.

As we become increasingly dependent on the Internet for our personal and professional interests, the Internet has proven to be an essential vehicle of Academic, Commercial, Financial, and End-users, which have greater impacts on our society. Although some long for the days when the Internet was used strictly for research and collaboration, the Internet must be recognised for its critical role in business today.

As in any other means of business, we cannot assume all the players will abide by a code of moral conduct. The mere fact that business is being performed online over an insecure medium is enough to entice criminal activity to the Internet. Many countries have a number of motives for taking steps to regulate the Internet. The principle aim of regulating the Internet is to create a legal framework within which all transactions can be secure and intellectual property rights are protected.

The chapters in this book are superb in intellectual quality and should be accessible to professionals, postgraduate and undergraduate students. Readers are welcome to join e-Centre for Infonomics at www.infonomics.org.uk for forum discussions on technology evolution and free subscription of International Journal for Infonomics.

Charles A. Shoniregun

1

Electronic Commerce Mediations: The Shape of Things to Come!

1.1 Introduction

This chapter looks at how the organisations use electronic commerce (eC) to generate substantial part of their profits; the current Internet cybermediaries are being evaluated as role models for the future. Following the trends for business process re-engineering and strategic outsourcing that emerged in the 1990's, many businesses are turning more and more to technology and the Internet to fill the gap of distance and education between the public and the product. Many organisations have turned to the Internet to market their products and others have even emerged as solely web-based. Before the adaptation of eC, electronic data interchange (EDI) has been used by businesses such as financial institutions, railway, airlines, motor carriers and shipping companies. These businesses realised that processing a large volume paper documentation accompanying shipment of goods resulted in significant delays in settlement and product delivery. Now businesses are relying more and more on information systems and information technologies. In order to gain and maintain competitive advantage speed is essential in product development and management decision-making advances. As these advances extend beyond the sphere of organizations to include consumers, industrial dynamics provide unprecedented opportunities for producers and services to bypass the traditional market intermediaries and interact direct with the final consumers. This move as has been suggested by early researchers, will lead to the gradual elimination of intermediaries from the value system [1]. Survey questionnaires and interview were conducted to validate some of the work that has been done by previous researchers, but as eC eliminates traditional mediaries, it has led to the emergence of new informediaries in their place. Informediaries are required to turn massive amount of dumb into useable information. This chapter discusses the outsourcing of an organisation non-core functions towards cybermediaries development and the enabled technologies.

1.2 Penetration of Internet into the Business Environment

Great Incentive to Survive

The penetration of Internet into the business environment changes the way of interacting in the market place and it has drastically affect the traditional link between suppliers and buyers, which provides a means of bypassing some of channel partners. These relationships include those with channel partners such as wholesalers and retailers through whom products and services are exchanged between the selling organisations. The Internet has aided cybermediation, and the paradigm has changed the whole concept of traditional trade by barter, it does not only revolutionise the marketing concept but also change the whole dialogue in which business will be conducting in the future. The Figure 1 below shows the diagrammatic illustration of cybermediation from meta-level. Furthermore, the diagrammatic illustration of traditional distribution channel and there intermediating layers, are depicted in Figure 3.

Figure 1: Meta-level of Cybermediation Wheel of Fortune

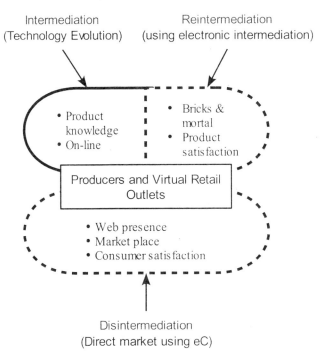

Intermediation
(Technology Evolution)

Reintermediation
(using electronic intermediation)

- Product knowledge
- On-line

- Bricks & mortal
- Product satisfaction

Producers and Virtual Retail Outlets

- Web presence
- Market place
- Consumer satisfaction

Disintermediation
(Direct market using eC)

In the global economy, there is a great incentive to survive and companies are planning to succeed to make their products and services less invasive even as the net becomes more pervasive. Companies are offering their products and services in a faster, cheaper, and more informative and more customer-orientated way, therefore, it is becoming more difficult for businesses to survive let alone prosper and grow. As the Internet becomes the de facto platform for doing business, it remains a vast frontier of 'untamed and uncontrolled' networks [2].

The traditional intermediaries (bricks and mortar) will continue to face increasing pressure for survival and large number will be led in elimination. Such firms provide matching services for buyers and suppliers in a traditional market. The eC-able intermediaries and clicks

17

are firms that conduct business using traditional methods and on-line interactive eC applications. The decreased transaction cost in electronic markets would lead to a reduction of traditional intermediaries in electronic value chains. Regardless of the extent of this claim, a thorough examination of the way that eC shape traditional market functions reveals three distinct and plausible scenarios for the future. The traditional intermediaries will either be driven out of the market (disintermediation) or be forced to alter their service, reshape their systems by adapting to the technological innovations and business activities and re-emerge in electronic market (reintermediation) while wholly new markets for intermediaries will be created (cybermediation). Disintermediation, reintermediation or cybermediation describes the dynamics of supporting value chain activities. Electronic commerce and the evolution of electronic market places have contributed to a continuous transformation of traditional value chain and systems. In more general sense, elimination of intermediaries appears to correspond with the emergence of Internet economy enhanced by the alleged move toward shorter value chain in electronic market places. The concept of shortening the supply chain in electronic bookselling marketplaces with particular reference to Amazon.com and Barnes and Noble, raises the question of whether there are indeed any strong economic incentives in other sectors of the economy to follow the eC trend. By driving out intermediaries who have been known to add significant cost to the value chain both producers and consumers gain strong economic incentives, thus increasing the profit margins of producers /or manufacturer [3].

1.3 Disintermediation Strategy

The Bypassing of Part of the Traditional Supply Chain

The concept of shortening the supply chain or disintermediation caused by eC is a relatively new concept. Disintermediation is the bypassing of part of the traditional supply chain that exists between the producer of goods or services and the consumer of those goods or services. The term 'disintermediation' is not new in the market and it is an ancient concept dates back to Spain's 15th century Queen Isabella and King Ferdinand trying to simplified the supply chain of spices from India by going directly to the sources [4].

The concept of disintermediation was later coined by the financial services sector to mean moving customer's savings out of banks and placed them directly with other financial institutions [5]. *What is the whole concept behind the disintermediation? Are there indeed any strong economic incentives?* By driving out intermediaries who have been known to add significant costs to the value chain [6], both producers and consumers indeed gain strong economic incentives, thus increasing the profit margins of producers while reducing final prices for customers. New technologies for eC on the Internet brought about the reduction of the transaction costs to the producers. This will enable the producers to internationalise activities that had to be purchased from intermediaries in a traditional market. An example is Dell's direct selling model, which completely gets along without middleman. With the growth of Internet enabled eC, disintermediation has become much more significant as the general removal of intermediaries, by the creation of networks connecting customers directly with service providers and manufacturers [7, 8]. The restructuring of the supply chain to gain a commercial advantage is nothing new, with intermediaries constantly manoeuvring to bypass their suppliers and/or distributors to shorten the overall chain and increase their profit margins. In the past, what have been the limiting factors for disintermediation have been distance and physical location. The supply chain for both goods and services was inherently bound to the distribution logistics strategy of arranging for the right quantities of the right goods or service to be available at the right place at the right time [8]. As setting up these distribution networks depended on physical locations, the effects of disintermediation tended to be localised. However, Internet based eC holds out the promise of removing the location based time and distance constraints of the supply chain from the producer to consumer relationship. A web site can be always open for business and can be reached by anyone with a web browser and a connection to the Internet. This shift from the marketplace to an online 'marketplace' [9] will lead to producers and consumers being linked directly to each other.

Internal disintermediation as provide the businesses to reengineer the business process by removal of employees who provide limited 'added value' to an organisations distribution channel. This type of disintermediation has been more widespread than external disintermediation, as far as organisations have started by implementing internal eC initiatives. After the first round of stand-alone eC ventures, organisations started to provide on-line access into their existing information systems (IS) applications and infrastructure. This has had a direct effect on the staff previously employed in customer service roles. The typical call centre operative acts as an interpreter between the customer and the IS system. If the customer can now access the same system directly over the Internet, the requirement for customer service staff is going to reduce. The effects of this were clearly seen in the success of the online stock brokerages in the late 1990's, which drew investors because of the perception of poor value from the traditional stockbrokers' fee structures [10]. This started as new entrants to the market replacing existing intermediaries, but once their success was recognised the existing market players disintermediated their own brokers to recapture market share and cut costs [11]. The perceived value that an employee adds to an organisation has been under examination since the outsourcing movement gained momentum in the 1980's. Even very successful telesales functions, such as at Dell Computers, market leaders in the late 80's and early 90's, have been internally disintermediated by online web sites [7]. Dell Computers, with its famous "direct method" and the Internet version of that, Dell Online, followed a similar logic by cutting out distributors and retailers. The public can buy directly from Dell, which cuts out the reseller's mark up and also keeps channel inventories low. This means that the computers in the channels are more up-to-date on average than those of Dell's competitors, thereby avoiding the problem of "fire sales" when new chips or other highly depreciating components hit the market [12]. As organisations open up access to the Internet for their staff, the opportunities to outsource information functions to new web cybermediary collaborators will grow. *'Who ever makes a product is looking at this new channel as way to go direct and eliminate some of the cost of the channel'*. OfficeDepot.com, cut a deal early 1999 with Hewlett-Packard Co. under which it could sell HP's Series 2000 printers exclusively for a short period of time, giving it a head start over its competitors in the retail channel. In exchange, OfficeDepot.com, which is one of HP's largest retailers, sent key marketing and customer data back to HP. Another case in point is the Home Point Corp., a start-up online retailer in Greenville, S.C., which has signed up more than 200 furniture makers and dealers to participate in its new e-commerce model [7]. The DTI (Department of Trade and Industry, UK) (2000), international benchmarking study shows that the following are the main reasons businesses move on-line [13]:

- Increasing speed with which supplies can be obtained
- Increasing speed with which goods can be dispatched
- Reducing sales and purchasing costs
- Reduced operating costs

Given the distribution channel or supply channel, consumers no longer have to wait for a retailer to open, drive there, attempt to find a salesperson may be generally ill informed and then pay over the odds in order to purchase a product, assuming the retailer has the required item in stock. Products and prices can be compared on the Web, and lots of information gleaned with a mere mouse click. A significant downstream channel (such as Amazon.com) has the following advantage over retail booksellers Barnes and Nobles. Barnes and Nobles are now offering personalised services: personalisation allows for the establishment of one-to-one marketing strategies where producers are able to address the needs of individual customers and offer personalised products and services made-to-order, production has become a feasible and attractive option for suppliers, mainly because of the ease of communication between supplier and customers. This trend is especially visible also in Amazon.com where for example, personalised copies of a book or can be created and delivered to customers with only a marginal increase to the production cost. The personalisation and direct marketing strategies are mostly expected to contribute to direct contact between sellers and buyers, thereby fitting within the disintermediation hypothesis [14, 15]. Consumers are basically in control of their terms allowing them readily to obtain information about product offerings and prices. Search engines serve to dramatically lower search cost for consumers that look for particular products and services in the global electronic marketplace. Amazon.com modified their cost structure by eliminating transaction, distribution, and product mix. The maintenance cost are use to provide individual pieces of information, to their customers twenty four hours a day seven days a week, with unlimited shelf-space that provides potential customers with accessibility to more than 3.4 million titles, that is more than traditional Barnes and Nobles. Amazon.com has customer added features, which helps to make information clearer in order to reduce the amount of search and retrieval time. The

Amazon.com has the following direct customer advantage over the traditional retail booksellers:

- 24 hours a day, 7 days a week availability
- Unlimited shelf-space that provides potential customers with accessibility to more than 3.4 million titles, 14 times more than traditional book super stores.
- Access to search and retrieval systems that ease the customer search job.
- Value added content as text excerpts and title recommendations, which can be provided to aid the customer in their purchase decision.
- Global accessibility from all over the world, on-line stores like Amazon.com can exploit the advantages of selling and distributing worldwide.

The easy access to information shifts the balance of power towards the end user. Although, Barnes and Nobles, are moving towards the electronic marketing as an alternative business and revenue models with shorter cycle times than previously. Barnes and Nobles, able to address the needs of individual customers and offer personalised products and services, to allow ease of communication between supplier and buyer. A lot of efficient mechanisms are helping to make a big change in the world of business activities (replacing inventory with storing data in database). Transportation is becoming cheaper with regard to posting and delivery. There have been notable cases of service sectors such as Federal Express, TNT Logistics, and UPS have emerged as major Internet intermediaries that utilise their logistics expertise and economics of scale in distribution to contract with producers in facilitating the logistics of direct sales, which also provides tracking and delivery information to customers. The driving force behind disintermediation revolves around the benefit to the producer, who is able to remove the sales and infrastructure cost of selling through the Internet channel [16]. Some of these cost savings can be passed on to the customer in the form of cost reductions.

The traditional trust intermediaries (for example, credit-reporting agencies) will only have a limited role to play in direct producer-to-customer electronic transactions, providers of eC platforms such as electronic mall (Bodense.com, and Emb.net). New forms of specialised intermediaries are expected to emerge, including public key infrastructure and certificate authorities. So some of these traditional intermediaries, most notably credit card companies will also have to resume new roles and responsibilities in monitoring and tracking electronic transactions between consumers and producers. New payment mechanisms secure payment producers (SPP) will provide the necessary infrastructure for trust building in electronic commercial transactions. It is expected that electronic markets will significantly alter the structure of intermediation in this case and the governments needs to be in a position to support the emerging market dynamics by providing the legal and regulatory frameworks that simplify and encourage eC transactions.

1.4 Intermediation and Reassembling Reintermediation

An Optimal Product Mix

The presence of intermediaries is easily associated with higher final prices for buyers; intermediation is emerging in the electronic marketplace to extend what we are familiar with in physical markets into the virtual world. For example, search services, matching, one stop shopping trust provision, information dissemination, risk management for buyers and suppliers, market infrastructure providers and distribution. Sellers determine their product offering based on signals they receive from the market. Intermediaries assist sellers in determining an optimal product mix by being able to receive and interpret market signal perception and changes. Intermediaries can directly assist sellers in their search for prospective buyers, by providing a major marketing and buyer targeting channels. Intermediaries can help buyers reduce their search cost by providing a single point of contact for information gathering and market transactions. A new type of intermediation may evolve from the unique capabilities based on the needs of the network market. This may involve breaking down the value creating chain of the physical market into separate entities or combine them into a different type of service. For example, retailers have functions other than distribution. A department store transmits a message that carries about the product and its quality. *Does a fancy website tell us much?* A web intermediary may sell quality information and nothing else. The toys retailer outlet 'Toys 'R' Us', not only distributes but also presents, line of products toy buyers are interested in examining and comparing. This indicates that an intermediary is needed if we are to avoid visiting each and every manufacturer of a toy item on their eC site. The Ford car producer in the USA announced a partnership with Microsoft in 1999 that will give potential customers a view, not just of their local dealer's lot, but also of what regional dealers, what is on order and what is being built. What Ford and Microsoft propose is merely a customisation of stock pipeline [17]. Some producers /or virtual retail outlets are developing the link between one-to-one marketing and mass customisation. Reflect was created by Procter and Gamble to develop online sales of beauty care products. It takes information from its customers and offers them cosmetics, all made to their specifications.

The eC intermediaries are needed for services such as deliveries, especially in the cases where sellers opt for 'contracting out' delivery services. The buyer has to transfer the payment to the seller in order to settle the transaction. This may involve payment processing and crediting. The intermediary is usually a third party facilitating or monitoring the transaction. The institutional infrastructure of markets specifies the laws, rules and regulations that govern market transactions and provide mechanisms for their enforcement. However, the key impacts of eC on traditional retailing systems are disintermediation of traditional distribution channels and eC reintermediation. Bailey and Bakos (1997) [18], explore thirteen case studies of firms participating in eC and find that, for the majority, new roles arise for electronic intermediaries that seem to outweigh any trends towards disintermediation. Although the sample is too small for formal empirical analysis, but it indicates that there is a general perceived increase in the role of intermediation services, (see Figure 2). In many cases, these new intermediary services will address the issues of trust and risk sharing that plague eC. New entrants may often provide the solutions, but because of need to engender confidence, established intermediaries able to adapt to the new environment may be well positioned. The demand for eC intermediaries will vary considerably by sector, but, in nearly all cases, they will be information-intensive and will exploit the information infrastructure to deliver the service.

Figure 2: An Increase Importance of Intermediation Services

	Sample	**Aggregation** Provision of one-stop shopping	**Trust** Provision of authentication and secure communications	**Facilitation** Exchange of messages between customers and suppliers	**Matching** Provision of marketing information to suppliers
Retail B2B	2	Yes	Yes	Yes	Yes
Retail B2C	3	Maybe	Yes	Yes	Yes
Automotive B2B	2	Yes	Yes	Yes	No
Automotive B2C	3	No	Yes	Yes	No
Information goods B2C	3	No	Yes	Yes	Yes

Source: Bailey and Bakos [18].

In addition, eC capabilities are giving birth to entirely new classes of business intermediaries. Forrester Research (1999), groups the new business activities under three headings: aggregators, auctions, and exchanges. These new activities attack different inefficiencies and provide different opportunity such as [19]:

- *Aggregators* : The aggregators create a business community: Aggregators pool supplier content to create a searchable one-stop shopping mall with predefined prices for buyers within a business community. For example, Chemdex serves this function for the buyer community of research scientists. These cyber-stores help geographically dispersed buyers and sellers find each other fast.

- *Auctions* : The auctions create markets and reduce sellers' losses: Auctions pit buyers against each other to purchase seller surplus. On the Web, sellers and buyers can participate in multiple, real-time auctions simultaneously–without accruing physical-world search and travel costs.

- *Exchanges* : The exchanges create stable online trading markets: Like stock exchanges, online exchanges provide vetted players with a trading venue defined by clear rules, industry-wide pricing, and open market information. An online industry spot market can operate at a fraction of physical-world cost.

Reintermediation is characterised by the functional decomposition of the overall sales transaction amongst several online services or intermediaries. This online intermediaries or cybermediaries, exist because they provide value-added services. These new cybermediaries fall broadly into three groups; those that have substituted an existing intermediary with an online version, those who have used disintermediation to create a new business and those who have added themselves into an existing supply chain [5] (see Figure 1 and Figure 2). As examples of these three groups, Amazon.com has substituted its online system for the traditional bookshop in the supply chain from publisher to reader. By having a wider product range than any physical bookshop and offering a customised 'personal' web service with access to information and reviews, Amazon is seen to have added value over the traditional alternative. *This distinction is becoming less clear as* Amazon *are now building the infrastructure to enable them to deal directly with some publishers, disintermediating in part their wholesales.* Dell founded their business on a direct selling model, disintermediating the existing PC distributorships and retailers, when they moved to an online business they continued this approach and also disintermediated service staff by providing online support and help pages. Auto-by-Tel with its car buyer matching services has actually added itself into an existing supply chain. The services they offer consumers to match their requirements to the existing car dealerships adds value by allowing the consumer to search collectively online the information from a range of suppliers. Reintermediation is reassembling an existing supply chain in new ways. Although this is not a new term, it has found popularity within eC where reintermediation refers to using the Internet to reassemble buyers, sellers ad other partners in a traditional supply chain in new ways [7]. This reassembling of the producer to consumer supply chain covers all forms of distribution, whether using electronic delivery mechanisms or more traditional ones.

1.5 Electronic Commerce Lowers Barriers to Reintermediation and New Entrants

Encouraged the Provision of Very Specific eC Services

There are a number of factors, which have helped tilt the eC marketplace in the favour of new entrants rather than existing 'offline' organisations. Internet based eC is 'new' and disruptive, and was perceived to be a technical issue rather than mainstream business, with its roots in computer networks and the scientific community. Mainstream organisations were naturally slow to take up the opportunities available, as the Internet did not naturally 'fit' their existing functional structure. When they did move online, there was a hasty rush of 'me too' eC initiatives which did not leverage the existing core assets and abilities of their offline activities. These two approaches, complete indifference followed by disorganised ineffectiveness gave the Internet innovators a head start.

The ubiquitous and pervasive nature of the Internet has been unique in allowing the early pioneers to leave the network access provision to someone else. Most other new technologies have been held back by the slow roll out of the requisite underlying infrastructure. In fact, most of the early Internet service providers were new start-ups, not the existing telecom companies. By the mid 1990's the low price and high performance of IT equipment coupled with the mass availability of systems software and programming tools meant that anyone with the ability and skills could develop quite sophisticated applications. When this group of software innovators met the Internet, they found a mass audience for their work and the more entrepreneurial made this audience into their marketplace. After Netscape released the Netscape Navigator browser in 1994 a *de facto* standard for user interaction came into existence [20]. These three conditions removed the high capital investment barriers to new eC entrants. This rapid take up of Internet access and its non-geographical nature, have given every web site a large potential market. This has encouraged the provision of very specific eC services that even with a small percentage customer yield are quite viable with such a large market. The more niches a market addressed, the more likely it is to find it on the Internet and being marketed across national boundaries [21]. This has produced a more 'level playing field' in the eC arena, with most (but not all) of the

27

traditional advantages of the existing players in a market being negated. The inertia of any existing organisation, which tends to resist change, had probably tipped the balance in favour of the more aggressive new entrants who have to succeed to survive, giving them the first mover advantage.

Promote Products to Suit Each Individual Customer

It has become clear that eC enables organisations to be much more customer focused. An electronic transaction is essentially a one-to-one transaction, and information about each individual customer's buying habits and preferences can be stored. This allows businesses to promote products to suit each individual customer and allows the companies to gain a closer link with each customer removing the traditional 'faceless' image. Apart from that, it is very important for customer service reps to be able to access and manipulate all the information involved in a customer's order. Current thinking is that eC will thrive, because many of the cost of conventional commerce can be eliminated. There will also be economies of scale, thanks to the huge numbers involved. It is thought that leading electronic business (e-business) will be to serve proportions of these users because of the global nature of the medium. Indeed, information technology (IT) is reshaping the basics of business. Customer service, operations product and marketing strategies, and distribution are heavily, or sometimes even entirely, dependent on IT. The computers that support these functions are become an everyday part of business life [22].

Many people are now spend more on books, CD, and Ticket bookings, online that they would in conventional shops. Online sales are expected to grow tenfold in the next four years. The act of shopping will be made so easy that barrier to purchasing, and in particular, to impulse buying will be lowered. The great number of advantages and huge competitive edge, eC has to offer businesses and the wealth of information available to both consumers, and businesses all at the click of a button. To further fuel the growth of the eC, the de-regulation of the telecommunications industry, hence the competition this creates will ensure that Internet charges are kept to a minimum. With some companies already offering a totally free Internet service, namely, Netscapeonline.co.uk, etc.

1.6 The Changing Nature of Disintermediation

Streamline the Supply Chain

In the past organisations practiced disintermediation to streamline the supply chain and their position in it. Backward disintermediation was when you eliminated your supplier in the chain (usually by acquisition or negotiation with the suppliers') and forward disintermediation was when producers /or virtual retail outlets bypassed their own distributors and supplied their customers direct. Amazon.com has no bricks and mortar but registered 8.4 million customers as against 1.7 million Barnes and Nobles, and 75% of all total on-line book sales whereas Barnes and Nobles has only 15% of total on-line book sales. Amazon.com has realised an enormous market value of $18 billion [23]. Given this scenario Amazon.com has a brilliant future to dominate the electronic marketplace as regard to books and CDs. Amazon.com senior vice president and general manager, Diego Piancenti has put the figure in to a global perspective, nearly a quarter of Amazon.com sales come from outside the United States and the number is growing. In the U.K Amazon has achieved a flying start by acquiring an existing and successful book selling business.

Many successful electronic-businesses (e-businesses) rely on a complex integration of IT support systems that can interact with many different channels. Databases, electronic mail systems, Internet web servers, personal computer networks and mobile phones are all part of the IT infrastructure for e-business. Managers must respect the hardware, software and customer in order to build a successful B2B strategy that fits into the overall corporate strategy and goals. The world's biggest technology firms – Compaq, Computer Associates, Dell, Hewlett-Packard, IBM, Intel, Microsoft and SAP – formed a Business Internet Consortium, which is a non-profit making organisation that aims to help generate technologies and practices for the growing e-business market. As e-business continues to grow, two distinct phases have evolved; 'brochure ware' on websites, and interactive eC [24, 25].

Now that the fear of being completely bypassed in the supply chain has receded, organisations are now adapting to non-linear supply chains where old and new intermediaries collaborate to effect producer to consumer transactions [26]. The threat is not that the existing supply

29

chain partners will bypass you or even that a new eC entrant will compete with the market share. The new threat is a collection of niche players combined into a competitor, or series of competitors, each taking a small part of the existing market - somewhat like being nibbled by a shoal of fish. For organisations structured to provide an end-to-end customer service, this partial disintermediation is difficult to compete with, particularly where effort has been put into developing a customer centric service ethos. *Will eC lead to organisations downsizing and outsourcing on a large scale* —In the traditional distribution channel, there are intermediating layers such as wholesaler, distributor, and retailer, between the manufacturer and consumer as depicted in Figure 3. A logical alternative to disintermediation is reintermediation, which actually points to the shifting or transfer of the intermediary function, rather than the complete elimination of it. Another reintermediation can emerge by differentiating the service of traditional intermediaries from online intermediation [21].

Figure 3: Disintermediation is Reintermediation by eC

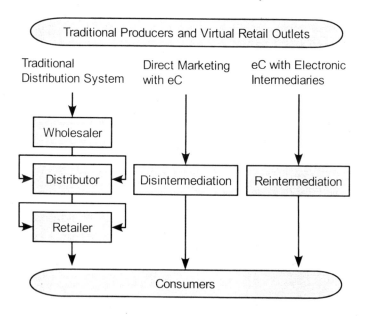

Producers and virtual retail outlets are in business to make money. A dynamic business model plays a critical role in achieving that goal. The environment in which Producers and Virtual Retail Outlets operates can determine the likely changes the business will face. The Internet stands to establish new game strategies for business as it renders existing bricks and mortar strategies obsolete while creating opportunities for wealth creation. To take advantage of the Internet entail conceiving and executing a good Internet business model. Such a model must not only have the right components, but also right linkages between them and its environment. It also must have the resilience and flexibility to take advantage of change.

Appendix 1 shows the diagrammatic illustration of proposed 'Producers and virtual retail outlets dynamic business model of eC implementation', which explores all possible factors. Furthermore, it is clear that the nature of eC and the change in relative costs it generates will cause a restructuring of the intermediation function, with some services gaining while others lose.

1.7 Outsourcing Non-Core Function and Internal Disintermediation

Embarking on Digital Business De-Construction Programs

In the business-to-consumer (B2C) eC market, the existing retail organisations are finding the online arena shaped by the new cybermediaries. They are beginning to leverage their considerable offline assets to help their online marketing and showing willingness to collaborate with or buy out these cybermediaries. Examples of this strategy include the John Lewis Group and Great Universal Stores who bought out Buy.com (UK) and Jungle.com respectively, to get access to the eC expertise they lacked. Other notable examples include Waterstone's bookshops contracting Amazon.co.uk to provide their online web site and order fulfilment. With such a strategic approach, these organisations prefer to disintermediate their existing IT departments and make deals with what where previously competitors.

In the business-to-business (B2B) market is showing an even greater willingness to adopt eC. Organisations are building on their experience of business process reengineering (BPR) and negotiating outsourcing contracts for non-core business services by embarking on digital business de-construction programs. They are seeking out cybermediary to partners to take specific services with the dual aim of reducing their internal costs by both outsourcing the function and exploiting the cost savings available from switching to an online format and also gaining a competitive advantage from the provision of an information rich service [27]. The network infrastructure to support this collaborative reintermediation is now readily available and there is growing support for extensible data description methods. These are enabling information to overcome its traditional limitations of a forced trade off between the width, the number of people who could read, understand and use the information. The more complex the information was, the less 'shareable' it became. Those organisations that can get their information spread the most widely will gain a competitive advantage. Given the experiences of many organisations first generation eC activities and following the lead taken by the B2C market, it seems likely that most existing organisations will look to external suppliers for their B2B software applications. The predominant need to be part of a bigger pool of collaborating digital infomediaries to achieve the critical volume to justify the investment, has pushed organisations towards third party services. This approach also falls neatly into the outsourcing of non-core functions approach currently in vogue.

Furthermore, wholesalers who in the past have built huge database are entering the online market, and offering their product direct to the online customers. Traditional retailers face increasing pressure from new entrants like Amazon.com who have successfully entered the market and developed innovative models of online retailing. In the software market, not only did the traditional retailers not disappear, but also many found the opportunity to enter the newly established online software retailing market i.e. Beyond.com. There has been a rapid growth of online auctions in various product markets traditional auction markets e.g. , auctions diamonds, coins and memorabilia or innovative online auctioneers e.g. Onsale.com, auctions almost everything, from computers to holiday packages. There are a few instances of suppliers that have set up auctions for their own products. In the travel industry, Lufthansa, started to auction out selected tickets. Not visible to the customer, however the fact that an intermediary, a web agency – Informedia is running the auction for Lufthansa) [28]. Before the Web, airlines could sell to the public over the telephone, but it was much easier to simply let travel agents sell to the public and pay the travel agents a commission to sell tickets. The travel agents had the specialised knowledge of schedules and fares, and people were willing to go to a travel agent close to home to find out the available fares and schedules. Following the advent of the Web, the airlines began selling tickets in large volume to the general public by making their schedules and fares available to anyone with an Internet connection. When direct sales rose to a sufficiently high level, the airlines cut commissions to travel agents from 20 percent to 10 percent, then to 8 percent with $50 cap for domestic and $100 for international flights, then, in 2002, to zero [29]. Travel agents responded by charging end users a $10 fee to book a ticket. This further reduced demand for travel agents [30].

Information, software, and content can also be delivered instantaneously, affecting the outbound logistics part of the chain. For example, firms such as Intuit now offer customers the ability to download their products rather than wait for a diskette or a CD to be shipped. This save the company in several ways: it eliminates the costs of the disks, the storage of information on the disks, and shipping costs. Some of those savings are passed on to the customer, who finds value in the timely delivery, in the lower price, and in the product itself. Most of the major record labels, including Capitol Records and Sony, have begun experimenting with the delivery of music over the Internet, perhaps in response to audio formats such as MP3 that promise reasonable audio quality over the Internet [31]. Likewise, by having more direct contact with end users, it may be easier to stimulate demand from the downstream end of the channel. This process has been used with some success in the software industry, where companies pre-release free beta versions and employ user input to improve and debug their product releases [32].

A structured interview was conducted among 30 organisations across the business sectors in UK. The accounts of interviewees, the 'untutored' responses to the structured questions, and the 'asides' followed up by comparing the interviewed. The interviewed were later used retrospectively to classify the experiences of the 30 organisations currently using on-line strategy to capture more target audience. In Appendix 2, we show the Strengths, Weaknesses, Opportunities, and Threats (SWOT) of eC from cyber-mediation businesses operations perspective. It is equally important to note that the SWOT analysis can

33

take place at any time in a business lifetime to find out the business current market position from the internal and external perspective

1.8 Technological Impact Of Electronic Commerce On Producers

Electronic Payment Solutions Are Increasing In Numbers

The technological impact of eC on organisation's business operations focuses on the electronic payment and the payment method negotiation. In everyday life, goods are paid for in a number of ways, by either cash, cheque or electronic payments, via credit or debit card. Businesses can often conduct payment among themselves also electronically through private network or by using Electronic Data Interchange (EDI), which is a 'generic term to describe processes in which commercial data is exchanged between different businesses computer systems'.

In the US, it has been approximated that 56% of consumer transactions were made by cash, 29% were made by cheque while the other 15% were made through credit and debit cards, and other forms of electronic payments. The limitations of these traditional payment methods are —the transacting parties have to be at all times in each other's physical presence. In addition, there are quite substantial delays in the payment process as detection for fraud, and overdraft and other problems have to be identified, and corrected. Electronic transactions in 1993 amounted up to 33 billion. Banks and retailers are seeking to *decrease paper transactions in favour of electronic transaction* as the processing overheads for transactions are both labour intensive and costly [33]. Electronic Payment implementations are one of the recognised growth areas in eC and vendors have been rapidly developing their systems to ensure competitive edge. However, as electronic payment solutions are increasing in numbers and sophistication, it is noticeable that information that was once in the public domain has been withdrawn now that the technologies are maturing for commercial exploitation. It is expected that until the market is stabilised, and specific solutions have acquired a clear competitive advantage, such a trend will continue.

Payment Method Negotiation

Currently there is only one visible method for payment negotiation: JEPI – Joint Electronic Payments Initiative – that has been launched by W3C. JEPI is a general purpose negotiation protocol based upon PEP (Protocol Extension Protocol) to allow web clients and servers to ask one another what extension modules they support, negotiate parameters for these extensions and ask the other end to commence using an extension if possible. It involves the registering of buyer and seller payment systems with a software module that implements the Universal Payment Preamble (UPP) protocol. This is used to determine if the other party has UPP available and what payment systems are installed. Once these are determined the client and servers can be configured, in session, to select (or provide options) for the must applicable payment mechanisms. This specific method is still under trial, but it is clear that standards activity within this area will be essential for a truly open electronic payment environment.

Credit Card Payments over the Web

Most companies collecting payment over the web accept payments using credit cards. The simplest approach is for the merchant to collect the credit card information via a separate phone call or fax and then to check the card through a call to the credit card company in the normal way. Merchants are required to repay fraudulent or unauthorised use of credit cards through charge backs. It is important therefore that every effort is made to minimise these charge backs, possibly by refusing business from high-risk locations, or by requiring a valid e-mail or physical address. At present the cardholder's liability is limited to the first £50 of a fraudulent transaction, and nothing else, once the card issuer has been informed of loss or fraud. Section 75 of UK Consumer Credit Act offers valuable extra protection to consumers who pay by credit card. For purchases over £100, consumers can claim against the card issuer as well as against the supplier if something goes wrong. Citibank is trying to encourage its customers to shop online and have launched 'ClickCredit', an Internet-only virtual credit card. Customers do not have to submit their real credit card number into cyberspace and will have a guarantee of their money back in the event of disappointment. What attracts the likes of Citi, to be so proactive, is the advantage of gaining an advantage over their competitors. They all want to dominate the market [13]. One solution for financial services companies is to outsource. In March of this year, Abbey National became the first large UK Bank to stop issuing its own credit cards. It sold its card operation to MBNA, the US specialist, for £289 million. The reason was that, after 5 years of selling cards, the costs of updating systems to compete with a full range of cards were just too high. This initiative is more widespread among large US Banks, but will become more popular elsewhere due to the high cost and speed of technological evolution [34].

To provide a more integrated service the credit card information can be collected directly through the Internet. In this case, it is important to ensure that the communication is encrypted to ensure that the details cannot be obtained by third parties. The encryption process used is normally the secure sockets layer (SSL). A more secure method known as SET is being promoted by card vendors but it is complex, slow and expensive. There are many schemes for implementing electronic fund transfer, electronic cash, and digital cash; however, none of them has yet achieved a significant market share. They can be split into hardware-based systems typically using smart cards and software based systems linked to computer systems. Although, throughout Europe, smart cards are now being adopted by banks, telecommunications companies, government organisations, airlines, railroad, urban transit agencies, gas stations retail shops and restaurants. The trends promise to grow, especially with Internet – eC transactions increasing. Smart cards represent the third generation of payment card technology replacing the embossed and magnetic strips. Although, these are being introduced to combat fraud, there are currently no firm plans to make them universally usable on the Internet. SSL and SET are currently the most common security technologies used, but given time will be replaced. Therefore, the smart card seems the obvious solution as it carries a unique digital certificate, which is a much more sophisticated form of security technology. Smart cards can be used in conjunction with any personal computer, mobile telephone or interactive television set. Card issuers need a strong business case before they will invest in the additional costs of providing the extra functionality needed for the digital certificate. American Express's 'Blue card' has been extremely successful in North America [35, 36].

Problems and Technology Use for Development of eC Application

The problems, which developers encounter, and the technologies they use for the development of eC application are analysed in the Table 1, and Table 2 below. The data presented in the tables are based on the outcome of 100 survey questionnaires conducted between September 2002 and April 2003. The survey question was conducted to validate the work of Kalakosta et al. (1999) [37], from the developers perspective and technological requirements of eC applications.

Table 1: Problems with the Development of eC Application

Problem	Not at all	Little	Moderate	Strongly	Do not Know
Data Security	5	7	3	80	5
Customers do not have access to networks	3	8	18	60	11
Lack of customers' confidence to use the Systems.	9	15	20	40	15
Reliability	9	15	30	35	10
Performance	3	15	25	49	8
Not confident for the value for money for such an IS	0	54	18	18	10
Lack of know-how	10	55	10	15	10
Functionality	3	25	54	10	8
Do not know customers' requirements	0	54	30	8	8
Lack of employees confidence	15	59	15	3	8

The main problem as expected is data security, which hinders the faster development of the eC applications. Financial transactions carried out in banks require a high level of security and confidentiality. Customers' accessibility to networks is also an important problem. Without the critical mass of customers who have access to the Internet networks and are familiar with the technology, eC is difficult to become

37

popular. This problem related to the next one, which refers to the lack of confidence of customers in using eC applications. Indeed, it is important to notice from the above Table 1, that employee confidence and customer requirements, specification are not considered as main problems.

Table 2: The Technology Requirements for Electronic Commerce Application

Technology Requirements	Not at all	Little	Moderate	Strongly	Do not Know
Data Bases	0	0	18	72	10
Public Networks-Internet	10	4	20	56	10
Data Warehouses	4	10	56	20	10
Groupware and Decision Support Systems with customers	4	18	34	34	10
Private Networks	10	4	53	18	15
Image Processing	4	19	49	18	10
Tele/Videoconferencing	18	18	44	10	10
Multimedia	4	61	10	10	15
Optical Character Recognition	18	18	50	4	10
Virtual Reality	62	20	0	0	18
Voice Recognition	20	65	0	0	15

Furthermore, with respect to the technologies used, Table 2 shows that databases are, as expected, the most important technology of all modern invention as data storage concern. It is a mature technology with approved applicability. Data warehouses follow in the third position, as they are a more recent development in the area of data modelling and storage. As eC technology concern, technologies like virtual reality and voice recognition have very limited use if any. These technologies, which are in their embryonic stages, require a more functionality with advanced capacity eC infrastructure. Optical character recognition is slightly in a better position but again with a very low percentage of usage at present time.

1.9 Explosive Popularity of The Internet

Technologies Is Evolving at This Very Moment

Generally speaking, the world of business is facing a dramatic change, often referred to as 'information technology evolution'. Its magnitude does not seem to be any lesser than the industrial revolution at the start of twentieth century. Advances in information and communication technologies (ICT) are the main drivers behind this evolution. Explosive popularity of the Internet as a business tool has created a new type of economy, which may be called 'digital economy'. This emerging economy is bringing with it new forms of IT-enabled intermediation, on-line businesses, virtual supply chains, rapidly changing eC technologies, increasing knowledge intensity, and unprecedented sensitivity of time-to-market by customers.

The information-technology revolution has barely begun, but is spreading fast. Over a century ago, technological innovations took decades to make their way around the world. The promise of significant growth has given the boost for eC to be a high priority on many public and private sector agendas. And to date, the growth has been fairly impressive. Starting from zero in 1995, total eC is predicted to reach an estimated $1 trillion between 2003 and 2005. These estimates are very speculative and rank amongst the highest of the dozen estimates generated by various management consultancy or market research companies. Another reason propelling the exceptional growth of eC is the decreased costs of accessing the Internet. The combination of technologies, the Internet WWW and browsers enable interactive media that allows one-to-many communication. Because each of these technologies is evolving at this very moment, today's Internet may very well become a different set of technologies and standards in the future. This both generates and encourages a large industry that supports and develops the Internet; it also explains why the current interest and enthusiasm for eC is focused on the enabled technology of eC. Thanks to these technologies, the cost and difficulty of eC have decreased, so that average people can routinely engage in it from the comfort of their own homes. Based on current experiences and judging from the various eC successes and failures to date, the sectors that likely to be significantly affected by eC *in the future* are as follow:

- Security
- Those whose products have a high price-to-bulk ration such as music CDs,
- Commodities such as routine business flights, and
- Intangible products such as software that can be delivered over the Net.

Products unlikely to be significantly affected including those with high tactile characteristics such as fur coats or high fashion clothing and expensive items such as jewellery. As eC evolves, it is likely to follow the 'reverse product cycle', in which process efficiency gains are followed by quality improvements to existing products and then the creation of new products. It is in final stage that significant economic growth occurs. Electronic commerce has the potential to be a platform from which significant new products emerge, many of which will be *digital and delivered online.*

While the new modes of conducting business offered by eC will generate growth, products and methods that eC presents will no longer be used and become displaced. Initially, eC may generate efficiency gains as new methods replace previous ones. In the process, businesses will fail and jobs will be lost. This is the natural evolution of economics, and there are many historical precedents to show that the economic efficiency that comes from this creative destruction is beneficial to the economy and will ultimately generate more growth and jobs. Electronic commerce is transforming the marketplace by changing companies' business models by shaping relations among market actors, and by contributing to changes in market structure. Electronic commerce also changes companies' competitive advantages and the nature of the company's competition. Given the dynamic nature of these processes, its likely the largest impact of eC will be on Small Medium Enterprises (SMEs) as many large businesses already have technologies such as EDI systems in place. Due to the relatively young age of the Internet as a commercial communication tool, more research needs to be done in evaluating what benefits the Internet can offer to SMEs. The major hindrance of eC at the moment is the issue of security. Transaction security is one of the most hotly debated open issues with various proposed solutions being put forward. At present consumers are still not fully utilising the Web because of security issues and low public confidence in the Web. Businesses will need to use encryption and digital signature methods to ensure that proprietary customers' information is protected.

The opportunity to small businesses to suddenly play on a world stage will encourage businesses to rethink their marketing strategies and sharpen up the unique proposition for products or services within their portfolio range. At the same time, they will be able to review production efficiency, cut costs and increase profit margins. No forward looking enterprise can afford to ignore eC any more that it can afford to ignore any effective marketing medium however, it is more than a marketing medium, it is in fact, a new, instantly accessible global marketplace.

Electronic commerce is in its early stages of adoption and is rapidly evolving, making predictions very difficult. Whilst total consumer online spending is still a small percentage of the offline total [5], there is little doubt about the impact, that electronic B2B trading will have on organisational structure. If the promise of eC intermediation is realised, it will lead to organisations becoming more flexible, with those who grasp the opportunity to become 'virtual companies' outsourcing all but a very small set of core functions. The standardisation of data formats, network interconnectivity and user interfaces are driving down the costs of implementing and administrating outsourced cybermediary functions. The trend for employment to migrate from large organisations towards smaller specialist outsourced service providers looks to continue with the rise of eC. Whether this will also follow the trend for temporary staffing via agencies is beyond the scope of this chapter, but as eC lowers the transactional costs of administration this seems a likely outcome. Furthermore, the main and most celebrated effect of the Internet on the value chain is a company's ability to carry lower amounts of inventory by ordering directly from a manufacturer and shipping directly to a customer. This argument can be extended to all sorts of value chain bypassing. The Internet Business models, by Paul Timmers (2000), was an important touchstone in understanding how the Internet affects the connected activities of the value chain. Timmers made the first attempt to classify the different ways of doing business in the Internet era and provided some preliminary categories, such as "e-shop", "e-procurement", and "e-mall". In some sense, Timmers was concerned

41

with a virtual value chain and how the Internet was affecting that chain [22, 23, 24, 25, 26, 27, 28, 29, 30].

According to Louis V. Gertsner (CEO of IBM), in his keynote address at CeBit'98, states that it is very exciting stuff, and the greatest changes and challenges are not in the technology. In fact, connecting to the Net is relatively easy. The big challenge is the fundamental transformation of the way things are done in the world. That is because networks are great levellers. They dissolve barriers to entry and neutralise traditional assets like physical stores and branches. Networks dissolve the boundaries within and between companies, countries, continents and time zones. It's not hyperbole to say the 'network' is quickly emerging as the largest, most dynamic, restless, sleepless marketplace of goods, services and ideas the world has ever seen [38]. By combination of traditional and direct customer, contact seems a way forward. Barnes and Nobles have adopted a new strategy to pursue the traditional supply chain with a new sales approach, thus keeping the existing relationships with retailers while dealing with customers in new ways. Producers can manage the channel conflict of distribution through retailers and direct to customers at the same time.

However, companies like Intuit have been very reluctant to sell their product direct to customers for the reason that they do not want to damage their relationship with their traditional sales channel. Nevertheless, they have adopted a new alternative by selling their product on the Web and in regular retail stores. In the absence of a multi-channel approaches a monopolistic supplier market (i.e. a small number of suppliers dominate on product or price) and the intermediaries are fragmented and have limited control over consumer behaviour, direct sales, wins and disinter mediation is the most likely outcome [39]. An example can be seen in Software and hardware markets where the dominance of big players (for example, Microsoft, Cisco, Dell etc.) means that intermediaries struggle and have to differentiate themselves through specialisation, offering services such as reviews consultancy and so on. Software retail has been radically changed by direct sales and digital distribution. New cybermediaries, such as Beyond.com, have struggled to attract customers. However, market or product knowledge of augmentation is vital; intermediaries can dominate especially through differentiation and better positioning in the market (reintermediation). Book retailing is dependent upon browsing and thus augmented search facilities as provided by the new on-line book retailers (for example Barnes and Nobles) have helped generate sizable customer base. Publishers tend to be fragmented and reliant on distribution channel with no or little experience of direct sales.

Intermediaries have protected against intense competition from outside the industry e.g. booksellers in Central Europe have been protected by a fixed price regime and the supplier market is fragmented, with consumers having preferences for unbiased choice, cybermediaries might seize the opportunities that the Web provides and offer innovative services. Purchasing decisions are complex and varied and the market is highly fragmented, cybermediaries can add value by simplifying information. Search example can be found in auction markets, where despite intense competition, cybermediaries like BidFind.com have quickly established themselves by providing value added services such as assisting customers in locating items in on-line auctions. It is often the responsibility of intermediaries to balance these needs. In fact, it is our contention that when a competitive market for intermediary services exists, an important service provided by a successful intermediary is the integration of the producer and consumer needs. There is a view that the ideal market for consumers is one in which the consumers are given complete, objective information about the products. However, for the producers, who prefer to influence the consumer's purchase decision, the best market is one in which they can provide biased information about their products. Thus, there is a tension between the consumer's needs and the producer's needs. Because providing information is costly, there is an issue of whose needs should be served by that information. Though it is sometimes determined by law, the majority of the time the retail intermediaries, through their displays and packaging, determine a balance between the consumer's need for information and a producer's need for influence. Ultimately, in a competitive market for intermediary services, a producer, which does not successfully balance these needs, will lose their suppliers and/or their customers.

The preceding discussion makes clear that the co-ordination role played by intermediaries in the exchange process is, in fact, a multifaceted set of functions, which are likely to be quite differentially impacted by any electronic service provided over a network. Network-based services may do a particularly good job in facilitating product search, but are less well equipped to offer product distribution (except of course for information and software products). Nevertheless, cutting out the middlemen also can cause new kind of problems like conflict in the internal relationship of producer with existing partner, called channel conflicts. An example is a company manufacturing expensive watches costing thousands of pounds, which in the past have used a wholesaler to distribute watches via retailers. Suppose if the producer decides to sell the product to the customers directly and if this wholesaler is a major player in watch distribution then wholesaler will react against the watch manufacturer selling direct. The wholesaler may even go to the extent of refusing to act as distributor and may pose a threat to the manufacturer by distributing only a competitor's watches, which may not be found over the Internet. Levi Strauss & Co. did not have much improvement with its original eC strategy, which shut out retailers from selling its blue jeans and other clothing online. At the beginning, Levis Strauss wanted to keep the Internet market to itself. However, within a year, the $6 billion manufacturer with a huge sum of several million dollars of investment on its online effort suddenly changed the strategy. Levis Strauss, decided to give up the direct sales on the Web, leaving online selling of its clothing to retailers like J.C. Penny Co. and Macys.com [7]. It may be the reason that manufacturer could not generate enough online sales to compensate its considerable online costs.

The ease of publishing on the web has facilitated the adoption of this technology by consumers and producers of goods alike. With the help of search engines like AltaVista, Excite, Yahoo, and AOL, consumers can obtain product information and often make purchases with much low cost of web publishing, firms can offer much product information through this medium than most others. This results in more product information, on balance, being supplied to customers than ever before, while on the other hand, the rapid development and diffusion of new manufacturing technologies in the last decades has produced a new pattern of product competition. Retail industry has been experiencing a dramatic rise in the speed of new product introduction, and a remarkable enlargement in the variety of models offered. In some cases, the speed of introduction of new products is such that some companies are willing to sacrifice their own market-leaders by introducing new models to prevent competitors from launching comparable products [40]. The chairman of Sony summed this up by proclaiming *"....my job is to make our products obsolete, before our competitors do"*. Other companies, like national Bicycle Corporation, are already producing customised products for targeted customers [41]. The greater the variety of products

44

offered and the greater speed of introduction of new ones, the more likely it is that each customer will be able to find a product that exactly matches his/her needs and more mass customisation becomes stronger. This will certainly sound new and attractive for customers used to the conventional mass production environment, where low costs could only be achieved through restricted variety, as described above. Lured by this new approach, customers are then induced to expect more frequent changes and great variety at lower prices from industry. This cycle creates feedback that leads to a more unpredictable and dynamic market, where small changes in customer demands, that could previously be ignored, now must be seen as competitive opportunities rather than a threat. Thus, in the future, in new market, industries will fight to offer the most suitable product to each one of their customers at the cost of a standard product.

Moreover, the power of the Internet does not come without its risks. An article published in the Guardian, on 20 January 2000 gave quite startling statistics produced from research by consumer organisations worldwide. It was found that whilst cyber shopping accounts for only 2% of credit card transactions, it generates 50% of complaints and when ordering online, one in ten items ordered never arrive. The struggle between freedom and control on the Internet is set to continue for some time. Electronic commerce security is still an administrative nightmare threatening to manifest illegal activities. Due to the sheer amount and value of transactions that are involved, to do business on the Internet, customers and businesses need to feel secure and reassured that the e-business environment is private. Like any other distribution channel, the web poses a unique set of security issues, which businesses must address at the outset to minimise risk. Since commercial activities have been growing over the Internet, the security of monetary transactions has been a major point of uneasiness for many who are considering joining this new modality of buying and selling. Electronic commerce lacks security and reliability arising from the issues of a 'complete trustworthy relationship', among trading partners. Customers will submit information via the web only if they are confident that their personal information, e.g. credit card numbers, financial data is secure. They are vulnerable to not knowing what the receiver might do with the information they have access to. They know there is a possibility that information could be used in ways, which take advantage of them or their organisation [2, 42].

It is well establish facts that the traditional security measures such as password and identification cards cannot satisfy various security requirements. Internet security demands attention at multiple levels. Various physiological and behavioural biometrics for the authentication of individuals have broader applications such as the control of access to personal computers, private files and information repositories, building access control, and many other applications. Although biometrics is still relatively expensive and immature but the technology has offers new characteristics such as fingerprints, palm-prints, facial features, iris pattern, retina, voice pattern and handwritten. Furthermore, the integrated multiple biometrics features such as fingerprints, palm prints, facial features and voice patterns to authenticate a person's identity and verify his or her eligibility to access the Internet are in the development stage. The biometrics devices will continue to improve, becoming even more accurate and reliable as Internet technology evolves. However, businesses must consider appropriate action, the cost of securing their networks, and to deploy an effective security policy and infrastructure that will include interoperability, scalability, and ease of use and proven solutions [43, 44]. Corporate officials must get involved to ensure that these security risks are not ignored. Companies must consider all available resources, costs and current systems when attempting to prevent security breaches.

1.10 Conclusion

Adopting Multi-Channel Approaches Is A Way Forward

The initial promise that Internet based eC was going to completely disintermediate all middlemen and intermediaries by connecting the producers of goods and services directly to the consumer are becoming reality as year past by and the issues it raised are not going to disappear. The Internet is not a fad nor is it a trend. We are at the beginning of the next business revolution, which is already changing the way we live, work and play. Over 30% of the UK and 50% of the US population are already using the Internet. We are expecting this to become a way of life in the future [45, 46]. Adopting multi-channel approaches is a way forward for producers and the opportunity to adopt technological innovation, reshape their system (that is alter their services) in order to move along with the new trend. In addition, the scale of change reflects yet another concept of radical new ways of carrying out business operations enabled by new ICT capabilities.

Indeed, most of the current business model did not take into account the hidden impacts of eC implementation on producers and virtual retail outlets business operations —the proposed Producers and virtual retail outlets dynamic business model will, bridge the knowledge gap. But in the future new organisations will be the 'orchestra conductors' and most people will end up working for smaller, tightly focused Cybermediaries [47]. These cybermediaries may even assume *public roles, assisting legal and regulatory bodies* for providing institutional support for electronic markets. The elimination of intermediaries invariably has its share of the problems. It is extremely difficult to generalise on the type of intermediation in any given market. Electronic commerce certainly adds value to both consumers and businesses as we have seen, but it also has its issues. Whether the value of eC out weighs the issues is a matter of debate. Nevertheless, it would be careless, if we as a society were to ignore the issues. One can only hope that as eC develops, some of the issues it faces are solved, so that eC can whole-heartedly be embraced and used to its full potential by consumers and producers. It is clear that consumers are still learning about electronic shopping, in a world where businesses are also learning. The compress SWOT analysis from 30 producers and virtual retail outlets will enable successful eC implementation more probable when businesses realise that strengths, weaknesses, opportunities, and threats, are all necessary issues set to be managed. However, *'is cybermediation really the future or risk?'* but to ignore eC is to allow competitors to steal a lead in what will be seen as a prestigious technological revolution.

References

1   Malone, T., Yates, J. and Benjamin, R. (1987) Electronic Markets and Electronic Hierarchies, communications of the ACM 30 (6), pp. 484 -497.

2   Shoniregun, C.A. (2003) 'Are existing internet security measures guaranteed to protect user identity in the financial services industry?', Int. J. Services Technology and Management, Vol. 4, pp. 194-216.

3   Nelson A. and William H. (2002) Building Electronic Commerce, Addison Wesley.

4   Sampson, S.E and Fawcett, S.E (2001) The Impact of Disintermediation in Retail Supply Chains, Paper presented at the POM conference, Orlando, FL, USA. Blackwell Synergy - Inform Systems Journal, Vol. 13, Issue 2, pp. 191-206.

5   Jalat, F. and M. J. Capek (2001) "Disintermediation in Question: New Economy, New Networks, New Middlemen", Business Horizons, Vol. 44, No. 2, March-April, pp. 55-60.

6   Benjamin R. and Wigand, R. (1995) Electronic Markets and Virtual Value Chains on the Information Superhighway, Sloan Management Review Winter, pp. 62-72.

7   King, J. (1999) 'Disintermediation / Re-intermediation', Computerworld, Dec 13, p. 28.

8   Pitt, L., P. Berthon, et al. (1999) 'Changing Channels: The impact of the Internet on Distribution Strategy' Business Horizons, Vol. 42, March/April, pp. 19 - 28.

9   Rayport, J. F. and J.J. Sviokla (1994) 'Managing in the Market-space', Harvard Business Review, Nov/Dec pp.141-150.

10   Bergel, H. (2000). "Predatory Disintermediation", Communications of the ACM 43 (5), pp. 23-29.

11   Gallaugher, J. (1999) "Challenging the New Conventional Wisdom of Net Commerce Strategies." Communications of the ACM 42 (7), pp. 27-29.

12   The Economist (1996) "Selling PCs like Bananas," The Economist October 5, p. 63.

13   DTI Report (1999) 'e-commerce@its.best.uk', see also UK Government, Competitive White Paper on eC, The Central Office of Information, Crown Press 2001. www.cabinet-office.gov.uk/innovation/1999/ecommerce/ec, (Assessed date 13 September 2002).

14   Chaffey, D. (2002) E-Business and E-Commerce management, Practice, FT / Prentice Hall.

15   McEachern, T. and O'keefe, R.M. (1997) Rewiring Business: Uniting Management and the Web, John Wiley & sons, New York.

16   Klien, S. and O'Keefe, R.M., (2003) the Impact of the Web on Auctions: some Empirical Evidence and Theoretical Considerations, International journal of Electronic Commerce, forthcoming.

17   The Economist (2000) 'All your', www.economist.com/fulltext.asp?result= R00000004&hitNum=15&booleanTeam=mass%20%20customization, (Accessed date: 10 April 2003).

18   Bailey and Bakos (1997) The Impacts of Electronic Commerce on the Efficiency of the Economy, OEDC White Paper; see also Block and Seger (1998), "Leveraging eC for Competitive Advantage: A Business Value Framework" Proceeding of the 9th, International Conference EDI-IOS, Bled, Slovenia.

19   Lief, V. (1999) 'Anatomy of New Market Models', Forrester Research, http://www.forrester.com, (Accessed date: 8 February 2003).

20   Pattinson, H., and Brown, L. (1996) Chameleons in marketspace: industry transformation in the new electronic marketing environment, Journal of Marketing Practice: Applied Marketing Science, Vol. 2, No.1, pp. 7 - 21.

21   Turban E., Lee, J., King, D. H. and Chunget, M. (2000) Electronic Commerce: A Managerial Perspective, Prentice Hall Publisher.

22   Keen, P (1991) Shaping the Future: Business Design Through IT, Harvard Business Press, p. 9.

23   Timmer, P (2000) Strategies and models for business-to-business trading: Electronic Commerce, John Wiley and Sons Ltd, p60.

24   LaFaire, D. (2001) 'Are you ready for B2B?,' EAI Journal, http://www.eaijournal.com/Article.asp?ArticleID=156 (Accessed date: 20 March 2002).

25   Finance On Windows (2001) 'Marketwatch: Consortium to address e-business challenges', Finance On Windows, Spring Special Issue, pp. 25-34.

26   Vandermerwe, S. (1999) 'The Electronic 'Go-between Service Provider': A New 'middle' Role Taking Centre Stage, European Management Journal 17(6), pp. 598–608.

27   Ordanini, A. and Pol, A. (2001) 'Infomediation and Competative Advantage in B2B Digital Marketplaces' European Management Journal 19 (3), pp. 276-285.

28   Financial Times (1998) 'Middle men deleted as words spreads', Financial Times, October 27, pp. 3-8.

29   Smith, J.J. (1999) 'Northwest Bypasses Agents', Detroit News, February 18, p. B1.

30   Afuah, A. and Tucci, C.L. (2003) INTERNET Business Models and Strategies, McGraw-Hill.

31   Business Week (1999) 'Music over the Web', Business Week, March 8, 1999, p. 78.

32   Garud, R., Jain, S. and Phelps, C. (1997) "From Vaporware to Betaware," Stern School of Business, STERNBusiness, Vol 4, No.2, pp. 20-23.

33   Kosiur, D. (1997), Understanding Electronic Commerce, Microsoft Press.

34   Desmarais, N. (2000) 'Body language, security and E-commerce', Library Hi Tech, Vol. 18, No. 1, pp. 61–74.

35   Newing, R. (2001) 'Problem need not be terminal', Financial Times, 18 April, p. 4.

36   Edgecliffe-Johnson, A. (2001) 'The top players in intelligence industry', Financial Times Corporate Security, 10 April, p. 18.

37   Karakostas, et al., (1999) 'Measuring the Electronic Commerce Impact on Customer Satisfaction: Experiences, Problems and Expectations of Banking Sector in the UK, International Conference on the Measurement of Electronic Commerce, Singapore, 6-8 Dec.

38   Gertsner, L. V. (1998) Keynote Address. CeBIT'98, Hanover, Germany; 18 March.

39   Clemons, E.K. and Row, M.C. (1998) Electronic consumers interaction, Technology- Enabled Encroachment, and channel power: The Changing Balance Between Manufacturer's Electronic Distribution and Established Retailers, Proceedings of the 31st Hawaii International Conference on System Science, IEEE Computer society Press: Los Alamitos, CA, Vol. 32, p. 8.

40   Sanchez, R. (1995) 'Strategic Flexibility in production competition', Strategic Management Journal, Volume 16, pp. 135-159.

41   Kotha, S (1995) 'Mass customization: implementing the emerging paradigm' Strategic Management Journal, Summer Special Issue 16, pp. 21-42.

42   Ratnasingham, P. (1998) 'The importance of trust in e-commerce', Internet Research, Vol. 8, No. 4, pp. 313–321.

43   Kelly, R. (2001) 'Secure- procurement', Finance On Windows, Spring Special Issue, p. 26.

44   Kare-Silver, M.D. (2000) E-shock 2000 —The Electronic Shopping revolution: Strategies for Retailers and Manufacturers, Macmillan Business Publisher.

45   Financial Times (2001) 'Net Figures: E-business at a glance', Financial Times – Connectis, March 9, p20.

46   Cane, A. (2001) 'Juggling genius of computing – Obituary Claude Shannon', Financial Times, March 15, p14.

47   Ashton, J. (2001) 'Prevent, Protect and Recover Losses from fraud' 5th Annual National Collections and Credit Risk Conference, Las Vegas Hilton Las Vegas NV, March 18-20.

2

Protect User Identity in the Financial Services Industry?

2.1 Introduction

This chapter looks at the effect of the Internet on the financial service industry and it has helped companies get closer to their customers, increase their market audience, acquire an important distribution channel and offer convenience and accessibility to their clients. It has become an opportunity to deliver a seamless client experience in a multi-channel relationship. Until recently, the only real restriction on the size and scope of companies was 'geography'. Now the technological revolution has removed this barrier to entry, we should not be surprised at the extent and speed at which new threats appear to the sector. The rush by organisations to offer their products and services online has left many overlooking the threat to security, which has been deemed as the main barrier to the development of E-business (eB). In the global economy, there is a great incentive to survive and companies are planning to succeed in making their products and services less invasive even as the net becomes more pervasive. Companies are offering their products and services in a faster, cheaper, more informative and more customer–orientated way, therefore, it is becoming more difficult for businesses to survive let along prosper and grow. As the Internet becomes the de facto platform for doing business, it remains a vast frontier of 'untamed and uncontrolled' networks. Accenture [1], predict that the 'Internet economy will top US$1 trillion by the end of 2002'. This prediction is yet to become a reality caused by the present slow down in the global economy climate due to the September 11 terrorist attack on the USA. However, no one can afford to ignore the presence of Internet economy or its future potential growth. Analysts suggest that there is no way of making the Internet '100% safe', therefore, organisations and government are forced to implement security policies, technological software and regulations in order to control unauthorised intrusion into corporate networks. This also discusses the Internet security threats in the financial services industry, and suggests possible strategic and technical solutions.

2.2 Internet Revolution

The Internet Is Not a Fad nor Is It a Trend

Having begun in North America in the 1960s, the Internet revolution is now spreading to the rest of the world. It is quickly becoming an essential communication tool for any business. There are many predictions of the number of online users, from the early pioneers such as Kalakota and Whinston [2] and Dyson, S. [3], to the even earlier Claude Shannon [4] whose contributions to the way we live our lives now and will do so in the future are only some of the work of the 20th century. The Internet is not a fad nor is it a trend. We are at the beginning of the next business revolution, which is already changing the way we live, work and play. Over 30% of the UK and 50% of the US population are already using the Internet. We are expecting this to become a way of life in the future [54].

E-business is exploding, and many companies are formulating Business-to-Business (B2B) and Business-to-Customer (B2C). The value of e-commerce, B2B and B2C is estimated at hundreds of billions of pounds. Analysts predict that by 2003, US Internet B2B revenue will grow to US$1.7 trillion [6]. The B2B marketplaces and online trading platforms are deemed to be the future of commercial activity on the Internet. Other research by Goldman Sachs, estimates that by 2004, e-markets will be taking 44% of all B2B revenues worldwide. The secret of attracting surfers on the net and turning them into buyers is the optimistic view that is driving companies into the virtual world. Last year, some industry forecasts predicted that more than 10,000 online marketplaces would emerge in Europe by 2004. Forrester Research, the American research organisation, estimated that Goldman Sachs, the Investment Bank, would capture more than half of all business trade conducted online [7]. E-Commerce is billed as a marriage of old and new economies, combining a few old rules and some new ideas! Successful B2B planning is an iterative process that includes planning, execution, promotion and assessment. Companies are changing dramatically as they strive to lower overheads and improve customer service whilst reducing costs and build a worldwide presence independent of the actual location of the company office.

Ed Zander, President and Chief Operational Office of Sun Microsystems [8], states that many people bemoan the net as an intrusive nuisance, but this network of networks is becoming less visible, a sure sign of its huge success. He also suggests that the Internet is 'going away' just like electricity and plumbing did in the 20th century. In years to come we will be able to do almost anything we want through simple appliances, hand-held devices and mobile phones. However, in the global economy, there is a great incentive to survive and companies are planning to succeed in making their products and services less invasive even as the net becomes more pervasive. Companies are offering their products and services in a faster, cheaper, more informative, and more customer-orientated way, so it is becoming more difficult for businesses to survive let along prosper and grow. Two million new web pages, 200,000 new access devices and 150,000 new users appear daily on the Internet, Zander predicts that the proportion of companies making more than 10% of their sales online will grow from 14% today to 61% within the next few years.

2.3   E-Business Strategy

The Growing E-Business Market

E-business strategies should NOT be designed to change the businesses companies are engaged in, but to change the way they do business. Businesses that accept transactions via the web can gain a competitive edge by reaching a worldwide audience at a very low cost. They must evaluate what their competitors are doing, what is happening around them and manipulate this, expand upon it and adapt appropriate components. Mary Modahl, [9] outlines Forrester's method for studying people's attitude about technology to determine who uses the Internet, calling it 'technographics'. She suggests, that "for companies to take the best advantage of the Internet economy, they need to understand who uses it and where their existing customers fit in".

According to Forrester Research, customers either have a positive or negative attitude towards technology, namely within three categories; early adopters, mainstream or laggards. One of the best examples describes how Charles Schwab, Stock Brokers, transformed itself into the Internet brokerage leader. In 1998, they offered all trades online for US$29.95. In order to distance themselves from other online brokers, they added an array of financial information and services their competitors could not match. Their strategy included targeting individual investors who would normally have used a full-service brokerage. The strategy paid off as it only took fourteen months to make up in volume what had been lost on lower prices. Charles Schwab is now the industry leader and the world's biggest online and discount broker [10].

Many successful e-businesses rely on a complex integration of IT support systems that can interact with many different channels. Databases, electronic mail systems, Internet web servers, personal computer networks and mobile phones are all part of the IT infrastructure for e-business. Managers must respect the hardware, software and customer in order to build a successful B2B strategy that fits into the overall corporate strategy and goals. The world's biggest technology firms – Compaq, Computer Associates, Dell, Hewlett-Packard, IBM, Intel, Microsoft and SAP – formed a Business Internet Consortium, which is a non-profit making organisation that aims to help generate technologies and practices for the growing e-business market. As e-business continues to grow, two distinct phases have evolved; 'brochure ware' on websites, and interactive e-commerce. With careful planning and cooperation with the consortium, successful management technologies, e-business strategies and technologies should evolve [6, 11].

2.4   E-Commerce in the Financial Industry

The Internet Offered the Juicy Prize of Lower Transaction

The financial services industry has been busy creating an e-commerce market, improving interfaces and developing applications with web browser technology. It strives to integrate these applications so as to offer a variety of different financial systems within a single organisation. The European online Brokerage market outpaced growth in the USA in the final quarter of 2000, and is on track to have more than 10 million traders within 2 years. The number of online share-dealing accounts in Europe rose by 13% to 3.74 million in the last quarter of 2000, compared to the previous quarter. According to a JP Morgan Chase report, this figure is forecast to rise to 6.3 million in 2001 and 10.5 million by 2003. Existing investors switching from traditional brokers, operated by major banks, to their online units have sustained the growth *(e.g.* Deutsche Bank *and* Dresdner Bank *have both gained market share and accounted for 60% of all new German clients in that period).* The past 18 months have also seen a flurry of announcements as each bank has sought to position itself within platforms and electronic exchanges. The rationale is simple the Internet offered the juicy prize of lower transaction and administration costs and the ability to offer a wider range of products to a large client universe. Banks also feel the need to defend themselves against new entrants fearing a repeat of the advances made by the likes of Tesco and Marks and Spencer. Justin Bull, Managing Director of e-commerce for Barclays Capital also suggests that banks are now focusing on those applications that can deliver. He says, "there is an awful lot of head-scratching in the industry as to where we go with all this" [12].

In July 1999, John Reed, co-chairman of Citibank, gave up day-to-day management to focus on the firm's Internet strategy. He saw the Internet as crucial to Citi's target of 1 billion customers worldwide. E-Loan, America's leading online lender in 1999, started their online service with mortgages, but now include car loans, credit cards and small business loans. They intend to offer personal and student loans in the future. They entered a joint venture with Vivendi (French Group) and Softbank (Japanese media firm) to launch a European operation, Net.Bank, which opened its virtual doors in 1996. Their operating expenses are about half those of a comparable traditional bank, so they pay higher interest rates on accounts and avoid services charges. The UK Cooperative Bank, although a small bank is very innovative and profitable. Its latest venture is an Internet bank called SMILE. Egg.com has been one of the success stories of online banking in the UK. It is run by Prudential, Britains biggest life insurer. Egg is now in talks with several European retailers about possible jointly branded products and is also discussing settling its technology in Europe. They have 1.45 million customers and plan to spend £40/50 million on advertising and marketing this year. Fidelity, sells 15% of its Individual Savings Accounts (ISA's) online. The Royal Bank of Scotland Group (RBS) is to use FreeMarket as a platform for the procurement of goods and services. The FreeMarket B2B Global e-Marketplace provides a range of e-Sourcing solutions to help businesses by streamlining the sourcing process. They are the first European financial service organisation to offer this service [13, 14, 15].

In the rest of Europe Internet madness is reaching the media. Online banks in Germany and France attract more customers than their UK counterparts, according to data from Jupiter MMXI. UK users spend on average 30 minutes per visit, compared to 43 minutes in France and an incredible 83 minutes in Germany. However, in Germany, all four big banks are online. Deutsche Bank decided in September 1999 to merge its retail arm with its previously distinct direct arm Bank24. Its arch-rival Dresdner Bank, is *slowing wearing customers off 'PC banking', by using its proprietary software on their own computers and into net banking* [13, 16]. The Nordea, the leading Nordic Bank, claims to have the world's largest number of Internet customers and wants to increase this by 30% this year. Out of their 10 million-customer base, 2.1 million use their online service [17].

Ready for the 21st Century

For a long time the Mediterranean countries have lagged behind their Northern European rivals, but Southern Europe is now home to some of the world's most technically innovative banks. *In Greece,* Novabank, *owned by Greek Insurance Group,* Interamerican, *and Portugal's* Banco Commercial Portugues, *opened their doors to retail customers in 2000.* Portugal is also gearing up for the e-commerce revolution, with many of its country's leading financial service providers clamouring for the latest IT systems to help stay in the market and to increase their share of it. In

56

Italy, Monte dei Paschi di Siena might be the world's oldest bank, but it is ready for the 21st Century. They have launched Banca21, as their contribution to the virtual society. Spain is trying a new initiative of encouraging foreign financial service companies to dip their toes in their market. Lloyds TSB online bank, evolvebank.com, has taken a 'phased' launch to select customers in Spain, after discussions with both the UK and Spanish Regulators. In November 2000, Abbey National, UK's second largest mortgage provider announced that it was on the lookout for allies in Europe. Their plan is to launch their Internet bank, Cahoot, in Italy [18, 19].

In Australia, Ecomm is the leader among online banks in the Asia Pacific. It is the retail Internet banking operation of Australia's Commonwealth Bank, and has over 1.2 million customers. Out of the four largest Australian Banks, 2.9 million of their customers do some if not all of their banking online – they embraced online banking more quickly than online shopping. Out of a population of 19 million, Jupiter Media Metrics estimates that about 6.8 million use online services [20].

2.5   The Threat of Security

Security Generally Relied on Users

However, despite all the hype of getting their products and services online, organisations have been faced with an even bigger problem, 'the threat of computer security', which is one of the main barriers to Internet commerce. The original Internet was designed for research not electronic commerce. As such, it operated in a single domain of 'trust'. While provisions were made to allow remote users to globally access critical files on computers worldwide, security generally relied on users' mutual respect and honour, as well as their knowledge of conduct considered appropriate for interacting on the network. Like any other distribution channel, the web poses a unique set of security issues, which businesses must address at the outset to minimise risk. Since commercial activities have been growing over the Internet, the security of monetary transactions has been a major point of uneasiness for many who are considering joining this new modality of buying and selling. E-commerce lacks security and reliability arising from the issues of a 'complete trustworthy relationship', among trading partners. Customers will submit information via the web only if they are confident that their personal information, e.g. credit card numbers, financial data is secure. They are vulnerable to not knowing what the receiver might do with the information they have access to. They know there is a possibility that information could be used in ways, which take advantage of them or their organisation [21]. This is more evident in the financial services industry where very few large transactions occur due to the lack of customer confidence in security. According to Huw Van Steernis, e-Finance analyst at JP Morgan, there is a high penetration for simple products such as current and savings accounts. As the percentage of online shoppers continues to grow, 'risk and trust' of online transactions will be the most uncontrollable issues that hinder the progression of Internet financial transactions. For this reason, it is unlikely that many people will want to conduct much of financial business online.

Risk and Trust

Risk is an essential component of trust, but it is unclear whether risk is an antecedent of trust, or is an outcome of trust. Risk-taking behaviour and trust behaviour are really different sides of the coin; what really matters is that the connection between risk and trust depends on the situation and the context of a specific, identifiable relationship.

Risk-taking takes into account the profitability of the occurrence of an event between parties and the difference in the anticipated ratio. The anticipated ratios can be either positive or negative emotional consequences to the parties. The probability of negative consequences will depend on how risky the situation is and the existence of security measures that can avoid the risk occurring. However, organisations and individuals vary considerably from one another in the degree of assurance they require before they will act in a situation that has the potentiality of dangerous or negative consequences. The following are the most common security risks on Internet transactions:

- *Spoofing* – because of the low cost involved in web-site creation and ease of duplication, illegitimate sites are created and appear to be normal.

- *Unauthorised disclosure* – hackers can intercept data during transmission to get sensitive information.

- *Unauthorised action* – competitors or even unhappy customers can vandalise and alter web-sites making them malfunction or become incorrect. This has become apparent for small and medium sized businesses because they cannot afford sophisticated security software.

- *Data alteration* – contents of transactions can be changed whilst in transit e.g. user names, bank/card details are most vulnerable [22].

As commercial activities on the Internet increase, consumers and businesses will expect that their use of network services is secure and reliable, that their transactions are safe, and that they will be able to verify important information about transactions and transacting parties. Many things we take for granted in normal buying and selling of goods and services, in the real world can not be taken for granted in cyberspace. In order for the Internet to be accepted as a viable platform for e-commerce it is necessary to establish a foundation of trust [23, 24, 25].

All of the above security risks on Internet transactions are burning issues of concern in the global platform. In October 1996 two 'consortiums': the Internet Law and Policy Forum (ILPF) and TRUSTe, were formed to help address the Internet's 'no rule' state. Whereas, ILPF focuses on Internet law, the nucleus of the TRUSTe consortium is to increase the level of trust between sellers and buyers in electronic/digital communications, particularly Internet shopping upon which both eC and mC businesses are largely based. The TRUSTe was founded on the belief that 'the greater the level of trust among the participants in a transaction, the lower the transaction costs'. We also believe that the greater the level of trust amongst the parties involved, the more confidence there will be in eC/mC business, and the more willing people may be to shop on the Internet and, possibly, the less risk there will be in conducting eC/mC business. The principal principles governing the TRUSTe include:

- *Informed consent*: Consumers have the right to be informed about the privacy and security consequences of an online transaction before entering into it

- *No privacy without appropriate security*: An inextricable link exists between the privacy and security of an online transaction. Privacy is impossible without appropriate security

59

- *Privacy standards vary according to use context*: No single privacy standard is adequate for all situations. Any standard to be considered should be in the context of 'the best business practice'. This appears to complicate the situation as best business practice varies from industry to industry and from country to country. What is more, corporate clients may not perceive it as the best business practice.

One question comes to mind. Do emC firms inform their customers about the privacy and security risks consequences of an online/real-time transaction before selling to them? The answer is negative. Customers experience most of the consequences after they have parted with their money over the electronic and mobile commerce websites. The new challenge is how to manage trust in an electronic environment. The building of trust models is hindered by the unfriendly nature of security technology. Dean Adams, a trust consultant and member of ECAF (European Certificate Authority Forum) states that the banks were the first to recognise that while you may see pounds and pence or dollars and cents on the computer screen, what you are really dealing in is trust, if you lose trust, you have lost the business, potentially irrevocably. The global nature of the Internet as a public network means that trust has even greater importance in the virtual world, than in traditional commerce. In an information technology age anything and everything seems possible. Cases of Internet crime and abuse are becoming part of our daily life. The following are some notably public cases.

Case 1: Masters of Deception (Hackers): A network of 1000 hackers who call themselves Masters of Deception (MoD) were indicted by the US Federal grand jury for committing what was described as one of the largest thefts of computer information and services in history. The hackers were severally charged with computer tampering, Internet fraud, illegal wiretapping, and conspiracy. The MoD broke into over 25 of the largest corporate computer systems in the USA, including Equifax Inc. (a credit reporting firm with 170 million records), Southwestern Bell Corporation, New York Telephone, and Pacific Bell. All the hackers (under 22 years of age) pleaded guilty, were convicted and imprisoned [26].

Similarly, Fortuna Alliance Company took $6m from thousands of people by deception, by placing advertisements at several websites and inviting thousands of customers on the web to invest as illustrated in Case 2.

Case 2:   Fortuna Alliance Company: Fortuna Alliance of Billingham, Washington, took $6m from thousands of people in an illegal investors' pyramid scheme advertised on the Internet. Fortuna placed adverts at several websites inviting thousands of customers on the web to invest $250 - $1750 with the promise of earning, at least, $5000 per month if they could persuade others to invest. The fraud was discovered and in May 1996, the Federal Trade Commission obtained a court order to freeze the assets of the Fortuna Alliance Company [27].

The case of abuse (the commission of acts involving a computer that may not be illegal but are considered as unethical) was also apparent when *Timothy Lloyd* abused the privilege of his office as the chief computer network administrator at Omega Engineering Inc., as explained in Case 3.

Case 3:   Timothy Lloyd's Logic Bomb – the case of a malicious damage: In July 1996, Timothy Lloyd, a former chief computer network administrator at Omega Engineering Inc., planted a 'logic bomb' that deleted the company's software programs, worth $10m. Logic bomb is a malicious program that is set to trigger at a specified time. Timothy was charged with malicious damage and stealing $50,000 of computer equipment, which included a backup tape that could have allowed Omega to recover its lost files. Found guilty, Timothy was dismissed [26].

It is not only a question of whether a site is technologically safe from fraudsters, but also whether it is trustworthy. Egg.com ran into trouble in April 1999 when accounts holders found they could look at others confidential details; a similar problem hit Halifax's online share-dealing service. These are examples where the internal organisation is at fault because of inappropriate privacy precautions. These are the kind of incidents that shatter customer confidence [28, 15, 29, 30, 31]. The risks, to which the financial services industry is exposed, are detailed in Table 3.

Table 3: Security Risk Exposures

Acts of God:	Malicious Damage:
Fire	Looting
Flood	Violent sabotage
Other catastrophe	Non-violent sabotage (e.g. tape erasure)
	Malicious computer operator
	Malicious programmer
	Malicious tape librarian
	Malicious terminal operator
	Malicious user (e.g., user who punches hole in returnable cards).
	Playful malignancy (e.g. misusing terminal for fun
Human Carelessness:	**Crime:**
Keypunch error	Embezzlement
Terminal operator input error	Industrial espionage
Computer operator error	Employees selling commercial secrets
Wrong volume mounted and updated	Employees selling data for mailing lists
Wrong version of program used	
Accident during program testing	Data bank information used for bribery or extortion
Mislaid tape or disk	
Physical damage to tape or disk	
Mechanical Failure:	**Invasion of Privacy:**
Computer outrage	Casual curiosity (e.g. looking up employee salaries)
File unit damages dick track	
Tape unit damages part of tape	Looking up data of a competing corporation
Disk or (other volume) unreadable	
Hardware/software error damages file	Obtaining personal information for political or legal reasons
Card, (or other input) chewed up by machine	
Error in application program damages record	Non-deliberate revealing of private information
	Malicious invasion of privacy

Source: Adopted from Martin J. (1973) [32].

According to a survey by the San Francisco FBI Computer Intrusion Squad and the Computer Security Institute, online security breaches and the financial cost of such trespasses will continue to grow every year. This is the sixth annual survey of over 500 computer security professionals in US organisations. Within the last 12 months, 64% of businesses surveyed reported unauthorised access of their computer systems, which is up from 42% in 1996. Of those surveyed, 186 were able to cost the incidents at a total of US$377 million in losses.

The FBI later announced that organised hacker groups have targeted numerous financial institutions during 2000. They estimate that more than a million credit-card numbers have been stolen to date. The problem is not the juvenile hacker, but the professionals and as more commerce flows into *cyberspace*, businesses are becoming attractive targets [31]. Online purchases are dominated by credit cards. According to a study by the Activmedia consultancy, credit-card payment is used in 98.5% of Internet transactions worldwide. In the USA, credit-card transactions over the telephone and web accounted for US$90 billion in 2000 with an average transaction of US$80 [32]. Europay, the European arm of card network Mastercard, advised that 6% of all fraud in the Continent is Internet-related. Credit-card losses on the Internet rose by £2 million to £7 million in 2000.

Organised crime is the main issue to face organisations. Credit-card companies and banks are spending large sums to counter the perceived risks of Internet scams, which in turn continue to be one of the biggest worries for online shoppers. John Briggs, Head of Banking Alliances at Earthport, (providers of secure online payment software) states that the perception is still there in consumers' minds that it is not safe to buy or sell on the Internet. The 4th May 2002, marks the second anniversary of the infamous *Love Letter virus* out break 'I love you'. This is now marked as the Internet's day of infamy, because the entire world witnessed destruction on a scale never before seen and it turned our attention to the importance of Internet security and the constant battle to keep virus and hacker threats at bay. Since then, there have been viruses aimed at PDA's, the first cross-platform and first peer-to-peer computer viruses. According to Srivats Sampath, President and CEO of McAfee.com Application Service Provider (ASP) "this is just a sampling of what we expect to see in the future as we further migrate to a digital society" [33]. The love letter remains among the most prevalent viruses circulating on the Internet today. It took only 6 hours to spread the worm around the world, causing an estimated US$7 billion in damages. The virus clogged corporate e-mail servers, and caused organisations to shut down their networks to repair the damage and prevent further infection.

2.6 Corporate Security Policy

Business Relationships

There are variety of e-commerce security policies, applications and technologies available. As e-commerce grows, more secure technologies are being developed and improved every day. E-business has four different components that build business to customer relationships. Together, these give the online store a personality and the customer a true shopping experience. These need to have a sense of security without creating a feeling of *Fort Knox*! Good business relationships are built on trust over time. More and more websites are addressing users' concern about privacy by disclosing their policies in open statements and requesting customers consent before collecting or sharing personal information. In the end, however, the customer is the single most powerful protector of his/her privacy online. It is the customers' voice and choice that will make the difference. However, without a thorough privacy security policy, it is not possible to spend money in a responsible and cost effective manner. The policy may contain many elements including purchasing guidelines, and statements of availability and privacy. They articulate the manner in which a company collects, uses and protects data, and the choices they offer customers to exercise rights when their personal information is used. Thus, customers can determine whether they want to make their information available or not. Research has shown that customers have less confidence in how online service providers and merchants handle personal information than they have in how traditional offline organisations, e.g. banks, handle such information [6].

Strategic Development of Information Security

Accountants, systems personnel and managers continue to struggle to maintain a grip on electronic security. No company seems secure, despite enormous expenditures on security, and many are confused about how to approach the problem. The result is that those involved often find themselves putting out fires and playing catch up in a sea of raging technology [35].

Security should be viewed as a component of a company's overall risk management strategy. Senior management commitment to strong cyber security practices can help ensure that security issues receive the attention they deserve. Computer security attacks can cost as much as $10 billion a year. An attack can damage data integrity, confidentiality or availability. Organisations must understand security issues and the potential costs. The concerns of customers are frequently fuelled by headlines drawing attention to the latest security breach whether it be Barclays Bank, unwittingly allowing customers to see other account holders' details or Woolworth revealing credit card details. Security should be viewed as a component of the company's overall risk management strategy. There is no such thing as absolute security; in order to be 100% secure, a system would have to be disconnected and placed in a case [36, 37].

"Only one in seven organisations have a formal information security policy in place and only 37% have undertaken a risk assessment exercise."

Source: Department of Trade and Industries (DTI) Reports (Manchester, 2000)

Companies need a comprehensive security plan for their systems and Hopswood *et al.* suggest:

"A systematic approach to developing and continually improving a web security system within the context of the overall systems development effort, and within the context of traditional accounting internal control processes and structures".

Source: Hopswood, W.S., Sinason, D. and Tucker R.R. (2000) [35].

Companies that use the Internet for business purposes should develop detailed security plans and implement comprehensive policies to protect themselves from potential risks. True security requires education of development of staff, development of management security policies and procedures and creation of a security organisation that enforces these policies [38]. Bill Pepper, head of security risk management at software consultants Computer Sciences Corporation (CSC), says that companies need to look at the level of business risk and then apply security accordingly. Even though banks and their service providers strive to install impregnable security systems and generally succeed, despite the occasional case, it is customer perception that is important.

2.7 Network Security Policy and the Technology Available

Absolute Security Is Unattainable

The major initiative here is to ensure that each of the following is addressed adequately:

- *Authentication*
- *Access control*
- *Integrity and confidentiality*

The Internet uses simple mail transfer protocol (SMTP) to transmit electronic mail and most business transactions. These have as much privacy as a postcard and travel over insecure, 'untrusted' networks. Anyone anywhere can intercept and access the information. Therefore, it is easy to forge email or use another person's name. Theft of identity is becoming the nation's leading incidence of fraud [39]. The first objective in improving security is to control physical access by limiting it to authorised individuals. Most applications nowadays rely on passwords, cards, personal identification numbers and keys to access restricted information or confidential files. The aims of providing security are to protect all aspects of the computer systems: hardware, software, data, confidentiality, computer environment and the Internet. To produce a secure system, the threats must be classified first. The following categories of security threats are encountered by the financial services industry:

- *Physical threats* (e.g. theft, vandalism, fire, war, earthquakes)
- *Accidental error* (e.g. programmer error, user/operator error)
- *Unauthorised access* (e.g. breaking into the system remotely/directly, access to data and output)
- *Malicious misuse* (e.g. programs – virus, worms, Trojan horses); users (destroying files, data corruption) and computer fraud (modification of programs)

These findings corroborate with earlier findings of other researchers. All of the above categories of security threat are of major concern to financial institutions business communities, the designers of networks and to society in general. A review of security control measures suggests that although the argument that 'absolute security is unattainable' is not disputed, security risks can be minimised by putting in place appropriate security control measures such as the following:

User Authentication

User authentication hardware and software is coming into use to verify the identity of the user. Systems that rely on IP (Internet Protocol) address verification limit access to users with a specific domain name or Internet address. Authentication services are fully integrated into the enterprise-wide security policy and can be centrally managed through a graphical user interface, tracked through a log viewer [40]. Because everyone has unique physical attributes, in theory a computer can be programmed to recognise them. Passwords, cards, pin numbers and keys can be forgotten, stolen, forged, lost or given away, but biology cannot. We have seen this used in the movies, and now we are seeing them on our desktops! Computer manufacturers are now building systems that incorporate fingerprint and eye scanner software into their machines so that companies can authenticate the user by verification of finger, thumb, palm, hand geometry, wrist vein, face, eye, voice prints, key stroke dynamics or hand written signatures. Biometrics could be a major security system for the future in the battle against online crime. It is basically concerned with digitally encoding physical attributes of the user's voice, eye, face or hand to a unique ID. Such ID is now used for clearance into a building by the FBI and it is hoped that this type of identification could be used in the future to secure online transaction(s) [41]. Research into this field is currently being carried out to see if it could become a viable option. The foolproof way of authenticating someone is by physical identification, therefore, making it impossible for fraud to occur (unless of course, the hackers turned to kidnapping!). Despite the fact that it would be an expensive process to scan every customer with a biometric scanner, many companies, especially the financial ones, will probably adopt this strategy anyway. Overall, the cost of biometrically scanning customers may be less expensive than the costs incurred by fraud in the long term.

Infineon Technologies AG and Veridicom Inc. have produced finger-scanning chips that can be embedded into a computer keyboard or mouse to verify authentication of the user by fingerprint ID. As technology becomes cheaper, it is not impractical to think that we may have chips implanted into computer keyboards 'as standard'. Keyware Technologies Inc. and Proton World International have in turn produced a Smart Card that can identify the authenticity of the user. When validity is confirmed, the smart card then allows release of credit card and user details to the website [41]. This technology is really not as 'sci-fi' as we imagine. Already ING Direct, Canada, has issued fingerprint biometric security systems to their online banking customers. ING Direct has distributed computer mice to a selected group of customers with embedded fingerprint chips. Results from trials will determine whether Biometrics is a viable security option. However, initially this type of technology will be very difficult to install due to the systems required for it and the expense of it. In the longer term, the costs should decrease and one day it may be possible for everyone owning a computer to have the technology for trouble free purchasing on the web.

The UK's Barclays Bank has been using finger scan technology for employee access to buildings since 1996 and is also currently involved in a pilot program for PC logins to the corporate networks. In 1998, Nationwide Building Society became the first organisation in the world to try iris recognition technology supplied by ATM manufacturer NCR. 91% of their customers said they would choose iris identification over PIN's or signatures in the future [39, 40] (see Table 4 and Table 5).

Table 4: Table of Biometric Technologies

Technology	Applications	Benefits/Barriers
Face Scan	Cheque cashing kiosk, time and attendance verification, ATM access	Facial hair can cause false rejection and this is highly dependent on lighting conditions. In addition, people generally do not like to have this picture taken, which could create resistance by consumers.
Finger Scan	Authentication for bank teller ID, customer ID	An inexpensive technology, although it can be difficult to read some population's fingerprints.
Iris Scan	ATM access	Very accurate under normal circumstances, though there is a high false rejection rate for individuals who wear designer contact lenses. Also iris scanning is quite costly to implement.
Hand Scan (Hand Geometry)	Physical security, time and attendance verification	Easy to use and easily accepted by users as this is not viewed as intrusive. Quite expensive to implement, and physiological changes in the hands can cause false rejection.
Keystroke Dynamics	In beta testing	Can be used with any device that uses a keyboard
Retina Scan	Network access, PCLogin	Extremely accurate and resistant to fraud, but requires the user to stand within six inches of the scanner. Also very expensive to implement.
Signature Scan (Dynamic Signature Verification)	Mortgage pooling application	Not very accurate because handwriting can change over the years.
Voice Scan (Speaker Verification)	Voicemail access, telephone banking	A logical choice for the mobile arena, though the false rejection rate is high

Source: Adopted from Meridien Research [42].

Table 5: Table of the Financial Institutions Currently Using Biometrics

Financial Institutions	Technology being used	Application
BACOB (Belgium)	Voice Scan	Telephone account access
Bank of Central Asia (Indonesia)	Finger Scan	Physical security
Bank United	Iris Scan	ATM transactions
Barclaycard	Finger Scan	Physical security and network logging
Chase (New York)	Hand Scan	Network login
Citibank (New York)	Hand Scan	Physical security
Charles Schwab (California)	Voice Scan	Telephone account access
ING Direct (Canada)	Finger Scan	Online banking
Perdue Federal Credit Union	Finger Scan	Standalone banking kiosks
Royal Bank of Canada	Hand Scan	Physical security
Wells Fargo	Face Scan	ATM transaction

Source: Adopted from Meridien Research [42].

Firewalls

Firewalls are the first line of defence against external threats. They act like a security guard for the company's internal trusted network, filtering all incoming traffic from the Internet (untrusted network). These generally implement one of two basic design policies: permit any service unless it is expressly denied; or deny any service unless it is expressly permitted. The first policy is less desirable, as it offers more avenues for getting around it. Depending on security and flexibility requirements within the organisation, certain types of firewalls are more appropriate [43].

Nowadays, most firewalls use packet-screening methods such as Transmission Controls Protocol (TCP) and User Datagram Protocol (UDP) that are based on predefined rules. Application gateways are more sophisticated and secure types of firewalls. These use services such as Hypertext Transfer Protocol (HTTP) and Telnet that, run on a server with two network connections, acting as a server to the application client and vice versa. They also prevent internal IP (Internet Protocol) addresses from appearing to users outside the trusted network. Additional firewalls are used internally by organisations, e.g. to cordon off servers in different departments [44]. The 'IPv6' was designed by the Internet Engineering Task Force (IETF), which includes a new expanded IP address, part of which has a unique serial number record of each computer's network-connection hardware. Every data packet sent will carry a user's electronic fingerprint [28]. However, reliance on virus protection isn't all that needs to be done. Employees are the most common vehicles for spreading viruses. Graham Curley, Senior Technical Consultant at anti-virus software company 'Sophos', suggests that employees are vulnerable and should be more aware of opening attachments including those from known sources [45].

Data Encryption

Data Encryption scrambles plain text using an encryption algorithm into an incomprehensible cipher text and then back to plain text again. This makes the transaction less likely to be translated if it is intercepted as it is transmitted across the Internet. It is the first and most basic form of e-security implementation, and it is applicable mainly for low value information transactions, e.g. email inquiries and sales correspondence. Many different types of encryption algorithm are available; cryptography, public and private key cryptography, Data Encrypt Standard (DES), Rivest Shamir Adleman (RSA), Secure/Multipurpose Internet Mail Extensions (S/MIME), Secure Electronic Transactions (SET), Secure Sockets Layer (SSL) and Digital Signatures. Cryptography makes secure websites and safe electronic transmissions possible. This allows online banking, trading and purchases by credit card to take place securely. The rapid increase in e-commerce must be supported by cryptographic security [39, 46].

Key Management

Key Management acts like a 'key' to access encrypted data. The sender and receiver of a message know and use the same secret key: the sender uses the key to encrypt the message and the receiver uses the same secret key to decrypt the message, known as secret-key or symmetric cryptography. Public Key Infrastructure (PKI) has been around since

71

1976 when Whitfield Diffie and Martin Hellman first introduced it in order to solve the key management problem. Individual users are issued digital certificates that accompany transactions. Businesses use this as confirmation of the user activity on their websites. The Diffie and Hellman [47] system gives each person a public key and a private key. The public key is published and the private key is kept secret, therefore the need for the sender and the receiver to share secret information is eliminated; all communication involves only the public keys, and no private key is transmitted or shared. Messages can be sent using the public information, but only decrypted with the private key. It can also be used for authentication (digital signatures) and other techniques. The secret key cryptography is referred to as symmetric cryptography. It is a 56-bit key, made up of 0's and 1's, dealing with encryption and authentication. Banks tend to use this method of encryption. The Data Encryption Standard (DES), was developed by IBM in 1976 and it has been a US Federal Standard ever since [39, 46].

Digital Certificates

Digital Certificates are electronic identification cards that establish an individual's credentials when doing business on the Internet. They are similar to a watermark on a bank note. They are used to verify that the author of a message is both authentic and that the message has not been tampered with. Anyone can send an encrypted message or verify a signed message, but only someone in possession of the correct private key can decrypt or sign a message [43] Financial transactions over the Internet normally use Secure Sockets Layer (SSL) and Secure Electronic Transactions (SET). Netscape developed SSL in 1986. It defines an interface in which a client and a server can perform data encryption, assure message integrity, validate user authentication and support digital certification. RSA Data Security have developed SSLv3 protocol for Java applications for use in banking, financial services, web publishing and customer e-commerce. SET was co-developed by Visa and Mastercard International Inc. They fully support SSL encryption. While SSL provides encryption for transmitting credit-card numbers on the Internet, SET goes further using digital certificates to verify the identities of both the customer and the merchant. The customer selects the credit card they want to use from an on screen 'wallet'. The wallet resides on their PC hard drive, which has a graphic representation of each type of card. After selection, the order information goes to the merchant, BUT the credit card data will go to the participating financial institution for verification. The merchant does not receive actual credit card numbers, only authorisation, so that credit card numbers are not floating around on 'untrusted' networks like the Internet. The Bank of America and Lawrence Livermore National Laboratory discovered that by using Financial Electronic Data Interchange (EDI), that they could transmit sensitive information securely and reliably over the Internet. Their results confirm that the Internet has the capability of transmitting crucial data, e.g. payment instructions accurately, even with current security measures. The Open Financial Exchange (OFX) is also working on developing online financial standards and solutions. It is focusing on the integration of XML into the client and server, enabling anyone with a PC and web browser to engage in e-commerce. The Financial Services Technology Consortium is also creating an electronic messaging format. It is focusing on XML and intends to make it the standard for electronic cheque processing via the Internet [39].

Virtual Private Networks (VPN)

VPN is another secure private data network that was developed on a public data network (Internet). Again, it involves encrypting data before transmission and decrypting on receipt. Extranet, is a secure private network that uses public data network to extend a company's private network to suppliers, partners, customers and other businesses. Data can be exchanged through an Extranet using EDI technology.

Gartmore Investment Management Ltd. recently introduced an initiative to review their technological infrastructure, by developing secure remote access for their systems in order to create a more flexible way of working. The goal was to improve the way in which staff access Gartmore systems from outside the company and to make working from home or on business trips easier, faster and more secure by protecting internal information from unauthorised access. Their Information Systems (IS) team has developed a system, which only needs a browser in order for staff to access Gartmore networks from any computer anywhere in the world. Initially the Lotus Notes system will be available, but they intend to extend this to all Gartmore systems. Dave Francis, Head of Infrastructure, says:

"Security was the critical part and there are two factors to good security: something you know and something you have. The system will work along the same principles as your bankcard PIN number, with a remote access fob, which displays a frequently changing number. The site will be accessed by a combination of both".

As a second security measure, the employee will be prompted to enter their usual username and password. Smaller extra security precautions include automatic shutdown after two minutes if the system is left unattended. Dave, like any other member of management, emphasises the fact that they can control the network for unauthorised entry but it is up to the staff to be responsible for their PIN number and fob. It is currently available to London-based staff, but there are plans to expand to their Jersey, New York and Tokyo staff [48].

Vulnerability Scanning:

Vulnerability scanning is a new category of software that has been founded by ex-hackers! The 'turned-good' hackers maintain an extensive database of all known vulnerabilities in systems and the vulnerability software explores websites from the outside to try and detect any susceptible areas. The software generates a report of these weaknesses and the group will make suggestions to a Company on how to resolve them. An example of an ex-hacker group is 'VigilantE' [49]. Vulnerability scanning cannot really be described as a tool or technology for security; however, it is a method of detecting flaws in company systems. The perfect way to catch a thief is to use a thief. These vigilant ex-hackers have put their skills to good use by forming consultancies as a means of making an 'honest living', doing what they like to do, but then also having the challenge of making the systems 'un-hackable'.

2.8   Alternative Payment Methods

New Financial Service Providers

Card groups are now being forced to invest heavily in 'smart cards' as they carry a microchip that helps prevent security breaches. Visa has announced plans to introduce chip cards throughout Europe by 2004. They have allocated £107 million to subsidise the costs of replacing terminals and upgrading banks' systems to cope with the new technology. Counterfeiting of cards alone is expected to double this year, costing British banks more than £200 million [50].

Smart cards represent the third generation of payment card technology replacing the embossed and magnetic strips. Although, these are being introduced to combat fraud, there are currently no firm plans to make them universally usable on the Internet. SSL and SET are currently the most common security technologies used, but given time will be replaced. Therefore, the smart card seems the obvious solution as it carries a unique digital certificate, which is a much more sophisticated form of security technology. Smart cards can be used in conjunction with any personal computer, mobile telephone or interactive television set. Card issuers need a strong business case before they will invest in the additional costs of providing the extra functionality needed for the digital certificate. American Express's 'Blue card' (Smartcard) has been extremely successful in North America. The French Banks have also started to initiate the program. George Wallner, CEO and founder of Hypercom, a supplier of retail point of sale terminals, warns that if the banks do not do something about customer payments, they will loose the business to the new financial service providers such as Tesco. He goes on to say that 'other' industries will find alternative methods, Internet based payments systems, e.g. PayPal. David Birch, Director of Consult Hyperion, an electronic payments consultancy is also concerned about the failure of banks to provide an effective customer payments infrastructure for the Internet [51, 52, 53].

PayPal is a new payment system that is capable of handling small-sum payments without generating bank commissions. It claims a current customer base of over 4 million, according to Media Metrix. PayPal users send purchase orders by email without having to wait for the bank to check the authenticity of account data. Qpass and Cybercash are also new micro payment initiatives [33]. Citibank is trying to encourage its customers to shop online and have launched 'ClickCredit', an Internet-only virtual credit card. Customers do not have to submit their real credit card number into cyberspace and will have a guarantee of their moneyback in the event of disappointment. What attracts the likes of Citi, to be so proactive, is the advantage of gaining an advantage over their competitors. They all want to dominate the market [13]. One solution for financial services companies is to outsource. In March of this year, Abbey National became the first large UK Bank to stop issuing its own credit cards. It is sold its card operation to MBNA, the US specialist, for £289 million. The reason was that after 5 years of selling cards, the costs of updating systems to compete with a full range of cards were just too high. This initiative is more widespread among large US Banks, but will become more popular elsewhere due to the high cost and speed of technological evolution [39].

2.9   The Internet Is So Vast and Difficult to Control

Regulation Has Been Brought to the Attention of Governments

The Internet was supposed to be all about freedom but, given this freedom, people manipulate it for self-gain. Regulation has been brought to the attention of governments and Professional bodies all over the world. The Internet is so vast and difficult to control; how do you govern something that does away with geographical boundaries and traditional, territorial based law? The unrestricted days on the Internet are numbered! Last year saw the start of what is to come in terms of regulating and controlling cyberspace. In the UK, the Regulation of Investigatory Powers Act (RIP Act) allows the police broad access to email and other online communications [28]. Financial fraud has been a serious white-collar crime problem for a very long time. However, in the Information Age, it is also a computer and Internet crime. In late 1999 and early 2000, a spate of e-commerce crime made front-page headlines [54]:

In late 1999, Visa USA wrote a letter to financial institutions informing them that a hacker had stolen more than 485,000 credit card records from an e-commerce site and then secretly stashed the database on a US government agency's website.

In January 2000, someone, believed to be a Russian hacker, identified only as Maxim, released as many as 25,000 credit card numbers stolen from CD Universe, an online music retailer. Maxim claims to have stolen 300,000 card numbers from CD Universe and allegedly attempted to extort $100,000 from the company. Approximately 2,000 records were stolen from SalesGate, including credit card numbers and other personal information.

According to Loxly Information Service, a leading Thai ISP, someone hacked www.shoppingthailand.com and stole credit card information on 2,000 customers. The police in the UK have pledged to work closely with businesses to help curb high-technology crime. They launched the National High-Tech Crime Unit on 18th April this year, which will train up to 80 officers to investigate cyber crime as part of a £25 million government program. In January 2000, Jack Straw announced that he was giving the National Criminal Intelligence Service (NCIS) £337,000 to draw up a detailed plan for a high-tech crime squad [55]. Again, perhaps it could be argued that governments are not necessarily tackling the problem from the right angle. If everyone knew the facts, they might ask why public money was being spent to protect sloppy businesses. The UK Terrorism Act was extended in February of this year to include 'cyber-terrorist(s)'; the definition now covers London-based terror groups who plan attacks here and abroad [56, 57].

In December 2000, ISO/IEC 17799:2000 was published as an international standard and the Code of Practise for Information Security Management. The UK Government sponsored the project. It aims to allow compliant companies to demonstrate publicly that they can safeguard the confidentiality, integrity, and availability of their customer's information [58].

In Europe, most people expect that information they provide to a commercial website will be used only for the purpose for which it was collected. Many European countries have laws that prohibit companies from exchanging consumer data without the express consent of the consumer. In 1998, the *European Union adopted a Directive on the Protection of Personal Data*. This directive codifies the constitutional rights to privacy that exist in most European countries and applies it to all Internet activities. In addition, it prevents businesses from exporting personal data outside the European Union unless the data will continue to be protected in accordance with the directive. *Under new EU Law, European consumers may now sue EU-based Internet sites in their own countries, and the rule may well be extended internationally.* The Council of Europe (41 countries) introduced the world's first international treaty on cyber crime. However, the European e-commerce market should become easier as the European Commission gets ready to eliminate layers of regulation and bureaucracy. As part of the move, e-traders will not have to comply with dozens of consumer protection laws created by member states. The Commission will ask member states to remove all persistent barriers to Europe-wide e-commerce, as well as changing from a sector by sector approach and transforming to a service by service one [11].

The USA, endorsed the gist of the Council of Europe's cyber crime treaty, which aims to harmonise laws against hacking, Internet fraud and child pornography. America favours self-regulation and sector laws. In contrast, the EU relies on comprehensive privacy laws that are enforced by data-protection agencies. Both agree that we must treat cyber space differently and that it needs laws and legal institutions of its own. Technologies to filter information will be introduced and the demands of e-commerce rather than governments will drive improvements. *The EU and USA harmonised a 'safe-harbour' agreement in November 2000, protecting companies from having their data flow severed,* as long as their privacy policies comply with certain principles [28].

The US Securities and Exchange Commission (SEC) regulates the US Securities market. In early March, they announced the fifth in a series of Internet fraud sweeps. They found perpetrators were using a range of fraudulent online techniques to raise funds for private ventures. The Regulatory arm of the US National Association of Securities Dealers (NASDR) issued new guidelines for online business practices when financial recommendations and advice is given. These will be treated no differently from those operating on the telephone or by mail [10]. An article published in the Guardian, on 20 January 2000 gave quite startling statistics produced from research by consumer organisations worldwide. It was found that whilst cyber shopping accounts for only 2% of credit card transactions, it generates 50% of complaints and when ordering online, one in ten items ordered never arrive. The struggle between freedom and control on the Internet is set to continue for some time.

As the Internet becomes the de facto platform for doing business, it remains a vast frontier of 'untamed and uncontrolled' networks. Accenture, experts in consultancy and technology predict that the "Internet economy will top US$1 trillion by the end of this year" [1]. The prediction is yet to become a reality as a result of the present slow down in the global economy climate caused by September 11 terrorist attack on the USA. Moreover, no one can afford to ignore the presence of the Internet economy or its future potential growth.

According to Graham Welch, Regional Vice President for RSA Security in the UK, "e-business can never be 100% safe". In his opinion, people are the main culprits. Financial Institutions are most vulnerable, as they are the easiest targets. Graham reckons that there is no way of overcoming the 'people factor'; security software solutions can only reduce the risks! He recommends continued testing, especially for the financial services industry [40, 54]. The growth of e-commerce will continue irrespective of the medium or type of environments established by organisations. The potential for fraud is much higher in the virtual world, although being able to access information from anywhere in the world at any time is perceived as a major benefit of e-commerce. Hackers and dishonest employees will continue to manipulate information for self gain, but if e-commerce is to become the dominant business platform of the 21st century, all the above must operate in a secure way all other things been equal [25, 59, 60].

However, the power of the Internet does not come without its risks. E-commerce security is still an administrative nightmare threatening to manifest illegal activities. Due to the sheer amount and value of transactions that are involved, to do business on the Internet, customers and businesses need to feel secure and reassured that the e-business environment is private. Businesses must consider appropriate action, the cost securing of their networks and they must deploy an effective security policy and infrastructure and include; interoperability, scalability, and ease of use and proven solutions [46, 61]. Corporate officials must get involved to ensure that these security risks are not ignored. Companies must consider all available resources, costs and current systems when attempting to prevent security breaches.

2.10 Conclusion

[handwritten: Questions will be asked to security & records at the time]

Information Age Terror

Trust in the electronic marketplace will require time to evolve. A good example of history repeating itself is the example of ATM machines in the UK. These, now ubiquitous, machines were introduced in the 1960s but did not gain popularity until the 1980s. So too, will it take time for Financial Services over the Internet to become a normal everyday occurrence [62]. But if biometrics are the way forward in making sure that all transactions are fully secure then the questions to ask are: *'How much will it cost to implement such security solution(s)?, Who should be trust with genetics information?, How long will it take the expert hacker(s) to decrypt such human genetic codes?* These are some of the concerns of businesses and online shoppers. Indeed, the human race has not only brought its business to cyberspace, it has brought its exploration of the psyche there, too. In the digital world, just as everywhere else, humanity has encountered its dark side. Information Age business, government, and culture have led to Information Age crime, Information Age war and even Information Age terror [63, 64, 65].

On a serious note, security will always be an issue for the financial services industry. All the measures proposed so far are not a complete solution but prevention. In our opinion, there is no specific solution at the present time for making online financial services secure. Moreover, *many questions concerning technology remain unanswered and frequently unasked* [66] by the customers.

References

1   Accenture (2001) 'Internet economy will top $1 trillion by end of 2001', *Financial Times*, 19 March.

2   Kalakota, R and Whinston, A.B (1999, 2001) *Electronic Commerce, A Manager's Guide*, Addison Wesley.

3   Dyson, S. (1997) Release 2.0: A Design for Living in the Digital Age, Broadway Books, New York.

4   Net Figures (2001) 'E-business at a glance', *Financial Times – Connectis*, 9
        March.

5   Cane, A. (2001) 'Juggling genius of computing – Obituary Claude
        Shannon', *Financial Times*, 15th March.

6   LaFaire, D. (2001) 'Are you ready for B2B?,' *EAI Journal*,
        http://www.eaijournal.com/Article.asp?ArticleID=156Accessed 20 March
        2002.

7   Counsell, A. (2001) 'On slippery ground: to B2B or not to B2B', *Financial
        Times –*
        Connectis, May.

8   Zander , E. (2001) 'When the Internet disappears you know it has arrived',
        Financial Times, 20 March.

9   Mary Modahl (1999) 'Now or never: how companies must change today to
        win the battle
        for internet consumers',in M.V. Rafter (Ed.) *The Standard – Intelligence for
        the
        internet
        economy*,www.thestandard.com/subject/book/display/0,4294,177,00.html,
        accessed 15 March 2002.

10   Labate, J. (2001) 'Downgrade deals blow to online brokers', *Financial
        Times Companies & Finance The Americas*, 2 March.

11   Marketwatch (2001) 'Consortium to address e-business challenges',
        Finance On Windows Spring.

12   Cameron, D. (2001) 'Online broking rises in Europe', *Financial Times*, 22
        February.

13   The Economist (1999) 'Online Banking,' *The Economist*, 4 Dec., pp.23-26.

14   Croft, J. (2001) 'Stepping from the Victorian to the internet age', *Financial
        Times*, 13 March.

15   Whitfield, A. (2001) 'RBS signs up to FreeMarkets 'b2b platform', *Finance
        on Windows* Summer, p.15.

16   Jupitermmxi (2001) 'UK online banking falls behind Germany and France',
        Finance on Windows, Summer.

17   Brown-Humes, C. (2001) 'Article: Nordea plans online boost', *Financial
        Times*, 22 February.

18   Hodge, N. (2001) 'Southern comfort', *Finance On Windows* Spring, pp.40-
        47.

19   Mackintosh, J. (2001) 'Abbey National sells credit card business',
        Financial Times, 20 March.

20   Fifield, B. (2001) 'An online bonanza', *Financial Times*, 8 May.

21   Ratnasingham, P. (1998) 'The importance of trust-in e-commerce', *Internet
        Research*, Vol. 8, No. 4, pp.313–321.

22 BT Trust Wise (2001) Securing Your Website for Business – A Step By Step Guide for Secure On-Line E-Commerce, BT.

23 Inada, S. (2000) 'Promotion of Intranet commerce through enhanced security', http://users.erols.com/sinada/commerce.htmlAccessed 4 May 2001.

24 Katsuno, M. (1998) *A Borderless World: Realising the Potential of Global Electronic Commerce,* Organisation for Economic Cooperation and Development (OECD), 7 October, pp.4–56.

25 Schneider, P. and Perry, J.T. (2000) *Electronic Commerce* Thomson Learning.

26 Keen *et al.* (1998) The Business Internet and Intranets: A Management Guide to Key Terms and Concepts, Harvard Business School Press, USA).

27 Business Week (2001) 'Gone but not forgotten E-commerce', *Business Week,* 22 January.

28 The Economist (2001) The internet and the law, *The Economist,* 13 Jan., pp.25-27.

29 Callan, E. (2000) 'Certificates: metamorphosis of cold war technology', *FT Information Technology,* 8 Jun http://www.ft.com/ftsurveys/spb212.htm Accessed 10 May2001.

30 Machlis, A. (2000) 'Software: security is far more than fending-off cyber vandals', *FT Information Technology,* 7 June http://www.ft.com/ftsurveys/spb20e.htm Accessed 10 May 2001.

31 Oreskovic, A. (2001) *FBI Warns of Growing Digital-Crime Wave The Standard Intellignece for the Internet Economy,* 12 March, http://www.thestandard.com/article/display/0,1151,22777,00.html, Accessed 15 March 2001.

32 Rodriguez, J.M. (2001) 'Card-carrying catastrophe', *Financial Times – Connectis,* April.

33 McAfee (2001) 'McAfee.com commemorates one-year anniversary of the infamous 'ILOVEYOU' virus outbreak with free virus scan and protection', Internet Wire http://www1.internetwire.com/release_clickthrough?release_id=26442&category=technolog, Accessed 1 May 2002.

34 Martin J. (1973), Security, Accuracy, & Privacy in Computer Sys, Prentice Hall

35 Hopswood, W.S., Sinason, D. and Tucker R.R. (2000) 'Security in a web-based environment', *Managerial Finance,* Vol. 26, No. 11, pp.42–55.

36 Coleman, K. (2001) 'Sensible security: how e-tailers and online shoppers can protect themselves', KPMG, http://www.kpmg.com/search/index.asp, accessed 15 March 2001.

37   Iwan, L. (1996) 'Internet security as part of the overall security plan – *Internet Security Seminar*, 2 April, http://www.ctg.albany.edu/projects/inettb/security.html, accessed 14 March 2001.

38   Merkow, M. (1999) 'E-commerce security technologies ec-outlook', 2 December, http://Ecommerce.Internet.com/outlook/print/0,,7761_253601,00.html, accessed 15 March 2001.

39   Desmarais, N. (2000) 'Body language, security and E-commerce', *Library Hi Tech,* Vol. 18, No. 1, pp.61–74.

40   White, M. (2001) 'Networking in a networked economy', *Finance on Windows,* Summer pp.82–83.

41   Chen, A. (2000) 'Biometrics – the end of online fraud?', *eWEEK*, 27 February, www.zdnet.com/filters/printerfriendly/0,6061,2444322-2,00.html, accessed 27 Feb 2002.

42   Meridien Research (2001) 'Forward-looking financial institutions should be investigating biometrics now', http://www.meridien-research.com/press/Prsearch.asp, accessed 27 February 2002.

43   Hawkins, S., Yen, D., and Chou, D.C. (2000) 'Awareness and challenges of internet security', *Information Management and Computer Security,* Vol. 8, No. 3, pp.131–143.

44   Madden, L. (2001) 'Great walls of fire', *Finance on Windows,* Summer.

45   Vernon, M. (2001) 'Insurance: no policy can protect against every eventuality', *Financial Times Surveys,* 7 June

46   Kelly, R. (2001) 'Secure- procurement', *Finance On Windows,* Spring.

47 ‹ Diffie and Hellman (1976) 'New directions in cryptography', *IEEE: Transactions on Information Theory*, June.

48   Francis, D. (2001) 'Gartmore remote access', *Gartmore Internal Magazine,* Profile No 28 April.

49   Anonymous (2000) 'Is poor security worse than no security at all?', *Computer Weekly,* 12 September, www.computerweekly.com, accessed 12 Sept 2001.

50   Mackintosh, J. (2001) 'Online fraud grows more slowly than feared', *Financial Times,* 6 March.

51   Newing, R. (2001) 'Problem need not be terminal', *Financial Times,* 18 April p.4.

52   Insley, J. (2000) 'If you shop with your mouse…', *The Observer*, 30 January, www.shopping.guardian.co.uk/howtoshop/story/0,5802,130839,00.html, accessed 30 July 2001.

53   Edgecliffe-Johnson, A. (2001) 'The top players in intelligence industry', *Financial Times Corporate Security*, 10 April.

54   Power, R. (2002) Tangled Web: Tales of Digital Crime from the Shadows of Cyberspace, QUE.

55   Sommer, P. (2000) 'Investigating cyberspace', *Computer Weekly*, 27 January, www.computerweekly.com, accessed 27 Dec 2001.

56   Burns, J. and Eaglesham, J. (2001) 'Police in new pledge to help curb cybercrime', *Financial Times,* 21 March.

57   Shrimsley, R. (2001) 'Cyber crime – covered by extended law on terrorism', *Financial Times,* 20 February.

58   Gamma (2001) 'Gamma Security Systems Limited: increasing confidence in information', IS 17799:2000, http://www.gammass1.co.uk, accessed 22 March 2001.

59   Chaston, I. (2000) *E-marketing Strategy*, McGraw Hill.

60   Dutton, H. (1999) Society on the Line, Information Politices in the Digital Age, Oxford University Press.

61   Kare-Silver, M.D. (2000) E-shock 2000 —The Electronic Shopping revolution: Strategies for Retailers and Manufacturers, Macmillan Business.

62   Jean Camp, L. (1999) Trust and Risk in Internet Commerce, The MIT Press.

63   Liu, *et al.* (2001) E-Commerce Agents, Marketplace Solutions, Security Issues, and Supply and Demand, Springer.

64   Whiteley, D. (2000) Information System Series, E-commerce-strategy, Techniques and Applications, McGraw Hill.

65   Timmers, P. (2000) Electronic Commerce (Strategies and Models for Business-to-Business Trading), John Wiley.

66   Preston, D.S. Dr. (2001) Technology, Managerialism, and the University, Glenrothes.

3

Multimedia Enriched Websites: Challenges to Copyright Law's Applicability

3.1 Introduction

Over the past two centuries copyright has survived numerous technological advances such as the player piano, phonograph recordings, motion pictures, television, radio, cassettes and compact discs. Often, these new technologies have posed challenges to copyright law's applicability. Although copyright has not always adapted immediately and smoothly, it has not prevented any of these technologies from thriving. Crime is crime, whether committed in the physical world or on the Internet [1].

The *raison d'être* of intellectual property right (IPR) is to protect the originators from unauthorised copying of their ideas and associated material for others' financial gain or general personal benefit. This brings into play one of the most complex and perceptively unclear areas of law. *How does one prove that an item of written work is original* and *How can an inventor assure the patent's office that the idea is his/her own and not that of a claimant from elsewhere?* IPR law seeks to define guidelines to address these and other problems, and to provide legal remedies for those who assert their ownership rights. Many of the

IPR issues existed before the Internet came into being; hence, we are in a position where due to the newness, unfamiliarity and evolving nature of the Net, pre-Internet issues are magnified many times.

The copyright issue concerning the Web has added further complexity to the problem of IPR enforcement. By nature of the immense global reach of the Internet, there is an inferred agreement that the Web is synonymous with "in the public domain" and that information posted on the Net is there for all to use. While this is a noble principle, it is perhaps idealistic. Together with education and entertainment, the Internet is also a business medium. For commercial and individual activities to be conducted effectively there is a need for protection of ideas and materials; examples of the latter include original print and music. This chapter discusses the impact of multimedia technologies, and the copyright of original print with particular reference to the music on the Net.

3.2   Multimedia to Web-Based Content

The potential benefits of adding rich media, such as video and interactivity, to Web-based content, in terms of additionally engaging the user, have been recognised for a number of years [31, 48, 44, 45]. This has been particularly useful in developing educational Web sites [44], especially in terms of demonstrating complicated techniques [57, 48], and/or for distance learning [47]. However, the effectiveness of such an approach has, often been hindered in the past by the technology available and infrastructure used; notably, the compression algorithms employed and the available bandwidth. These are discussed below:

3.2.1   Bandwidth

Faster Speeds Can Be Achieved

Available bandwidth can be affected by network congestion and is usually more restricted between a user's Internet service provider (ISP) and their local machine rather than over the Internet backbone [20]. This is particularly the case if the user is connected by means of a dial-up modem (typically at speeds of 28.8, 33.6 or 56 kbps, although the actual bit rate achieved is often considerably less [71]). Using a 28.8 K modem, it takes around five minutes to download 1 MB of data [76], which would represent a small amount of video or audio content, even after compression. A significant number of people connected to the Internet use dial-up connections [71, 35, 70]. In fact, comparatively recently it had been reported that most used a connection speed of 28.8 kbps [35]. Faster speeds can be achieved using an ISDN, xDSL, cable modem (up to 3 Mbps), satellite (up to 400 kbps), wireless (up to 800 kbps) or T1 connection [20, 23].

3.2.2   Compression

Video Image Quality and the Amount of Compression

Compression algorithms used for storage and transmission of audio and video tend to be lossy [20]. There is a trade-off between video image quality and the amount of compression required to satisfy a given bandwidth, so compromises must be made with respect to video characteristics during encoding [67].

3.2.3   Video Over The Internet

A Comparison of Transmission Modes

Unlike text, continuous media streams, such as combined digital video and audio, need "to be delivered in a predictable, synchronised manner" [21]. Wu et al. (2001) state that there are two possible mechanisms involved in the transmission of stored video content over the Web [83]:

- Download mode: One advantage of this approach, where content is downloaded in its entirety to the user's hard disk before playing out, is that it is more straightforward for the content provider to make available a file type that the user can play on their local machine regardless of their platform/operating system. In addition, the quality of the media received by the client machine is practically as good as that on the server and can be stored by the client for reuse. Low cost of set up is also a benefit, as a standard Web server can be used for delivery, and less bandwidth, editing and compression are required [20]. Disadvantages are the often unacceptable, delay for the user [55, 70, 83], which tends to preclude this option, issues of copyright protection [23] and the space occupied on the user's hard drive by the media [55, 28].

- Streaming mode: In streaming mode, part of the content can be viewed while the remainder is still being received and decoded (real-time transfer) [83], significantly reducing delay for the user in previewing the material. However, the duration of streaming is standard (real-time) for a given media file and if the bit rate threatens to overtake the connection speed, deterioration results to prevent this, sometimes to the point of stopping playout altogether [42]. Loss of packets, and therefore quality, is typical with this type of Internet transmission [42], because streaming has requirements in terms of bandwidth, delay and loss [83], and is therefore particularly affected by congestion on the network or a low connection speed [33]. Lin *et al.* (2001) note that real-time delivery does not occur with some applications, where, for example, the video might be cached on the user's hard drive for viewing at a subsequent time (progressive download) [53]. However, 'true' streaming files are essentially disposable [20]. This can be annoying for the user as the file can only be viewed once [20], but is good in terms of copyright protection [24], as only a determined hacker would be able to copy the file [42, 23], particularly if it was buffered in the RAM, as this is purged once the content is played [37]. True streaming therefore does not require the user to have large amounts of disk space available, as it is not stored locally [55, 28], which is especially useful where long movies are concerned [32, 42]. Streaming media formats tend to be proprietary file types, many of which can be incompatible with the user's system/player [20] and transmission often requires transmission over UDP, which cannot usually pass through a firewall [33]. In these cases, streaming could take place via HTTP as the firewalls usually allow TCP/IP traffic [79]. In HTTP tunnelling, RTP packets can be embedded inside HTTP packets, which can be streamed through the standard

HTTP port (80) and therefore through firewalls; however, this does have implications in terms of requiring extra bandwidth [42].

Real-time playback is achieved by buffering of the first section of the video bit stream on the client (usually on the hard disk) [30] to allow for decoding at the right time [62]. The duration of buffering varies according to delays in the network, size of the buffer and acceptable user waiting time, and the situation is further complicated by variable bit rate (VBR) encoding [62]. The player, which can be stand-alone or integrated into a browser as a plug-in, manages the content as a smooth stream from the buffer [49, 80]. Good compression techniques are required with true streaming to maintain a low bit rate, which can be difficult and expensive [42]. Additional costs will also be associated with setting up a streaming server [33, 58] and for improved editing [20]. Compared with TV broadcasting, streaming media has the advantage of VCR-like interactivity so that the user can access any portion of the media [78, 23], even if it has not yet been transmitted. This is not available with progressive download. True streaming also provides support for multicasting and broadcasting. This means that more than one viewer can access a single stream as opposed to unicasting [42]:

- Live streaming: In addition to streaming on-demand (pull – where the content is stored on the server), media can also be streamed live (push), which has the additional requirement that the content is encoded as it is captured [28]. True streaming is the only option for live broadcasts over the Internet/intranets [42].

- Progressive download: Progressive download, also referred to as pseudo streaming, quasi-streaming, HTTP streaming, fast start or serverless streaming, is an intermediate type of transfer between download and 'true' streaming that may provide the best of both worlds [33]. The content can be played as it is received, although the Web server has little control over the rate of data transfer over the network [28]. The download is therefore transferred at the speed available [79]. The consequence of this is that the player can run out of content, as re-buffering becomes necessary, causing playout to stop [28]. However, again, a specialised dedicated streaming server is not required [58].

89

Further advantages of progressive download are that the user has an opportunity to preview the file before downloading the entire clip [70] and, as the media is saved locally, can play the clip back more then once [58]. In addition, once the clip has been downloaded it is possible to access any part of the media immediately without re-buffering (unlike true streaming) [58]. However, there could be a reasonable delay in obtaining the media in the first place [79]. Again, progressive download presents problems in terms of copyright protection [37, 58, 63] and availability of hard disk space [58]. However, the author would consider that it is arguably easier for the user to delete such saved files when clearing offline content from their browser than having to remember the location to which they have downloaded them. The user would not need to have UDP traffic enabled/a firewall disabled on their local machine, although at busy times, playback would be slow and interrupted by pauses, which could be frustrating. Quality would be potentially high [79], as with normal download-and-play, as dropped and damaged packets are resent, unlike with true streaming [42, 59]. Progressive download is recommended for short clips of high quality of up to 2 to 3 minutes' duration. It is not indicated for live transmissions or streaming files to large numbers of users at a time as it does not support broadcasting or multicasting. In addition, viewers are not able to access portions of the media ahead of those, which have already been downloaded [42]. Progressive download can make use of more efficient two-pass VBR encoding. However, it is not suitable for mobile devices as they lack the required storage [63]. Gulie concluded that for streaming on demand it is completely reasonable to use either true streaming or progressive download technologies, since they both have their benefits [42].

3.3   Codecs for Low Bit Rate Applications

Audio File Size Can Be Reduced Significantly

Apart from editing, audio file size can be reduced significantly by choosing or converting to a mono source (which is usually acceptable for speech) [42], compressing for voice quality, reducing the sampling rate (down to 8 KHz is probably acceptable for speech [23]) and reducing the bit depth (say from 16 down to 8 or even 4 bits, which again is not a problem for speech [42]). There are a large number of audio codec standards available for compressing/decompressing audio files [13], although many of these are unsuitable for streaming content at low bit rates. Audio, on the whole, requires significantly less bandwidth than acceptable video, and files are generally compressed for either voice or music, to varying levels of quality. Music typically requires more storage and a higher bit rate than speech, especially for stereo content [79]. The potential for downloading audio content is well publicised, particularly following the Napster controversy, with perhaps the best-known codec used being the MP3 format. Unlike its name suggests, MP3 actually refers to MPEG-1 layer 3 audio rather than MPEG-3 (which has been abandoned; [42]). However, MP3 files require a bit rate of 64 kbps (128 for stereo) so can not be streamed over dial-up modem connections, especially if combined with video [23]. Audio codecs for speech have been developed on the basis of psychoacoustics, modelling of the human voice (including from military research and use) and statistical (waveform) redundancy [23]. Those available for streaming over low bit rates include Qualcomm PureVoice (which can be compressed down to 7 kbps for speech and is particularly recommended for streaming use) [79], ADPCM (or G.726)(32 kbps), GSM [23], DVM, G.723 [85] and DVI [68, 19]. The proprietary formats, RealAudio and Windows Media 8, are additional options [79]:

- Video File Size: Besides editing, video file size can be reduced significantly by lowering the frame rate (temporal scaling), reducing the dimensions of the window in which the video is displayed (spatial scaling), adjusting the colour resolution and using compression [23]. The video capture card usually results in some preliminary encoding (compression) of the content compared with the original source [75]. Typical spatial scaling for low bit rate video necessitates a reduction of the resolution from 720 x 576 pixels down to at least 176 x 144 pixels, which is known as QCIF (Quarter Common Interface Format) or even a Sub-QCIF 128 x 96, thumbnail size window [85, 68]. Many of the codecs work on macroblocks of 8 x 8 pixels [29] and the aspect ratio should therefore be a multiple of 16 [24, 42].

In addition, the frame rate can be reduced [70], often to 15 frames per second (fps) or less [72, 80], usually from a standard 24, 25 or 30. Colour resolution sub-sampling (YUV) often occurs during

91

capture [23]. Any additional data reduction can be achieved through compression. Dipert cites a "narrowband-streaming scenario" as QCIF resolution, 15 fps and an approximate bit rate of 34 kbps [36]. Masry and Hemami analysed subjective quality of low bit rate video evaluated at 352x240 pixels up to rates of 30 fps [56]. Gulie advises setting a conservative data rate as codecs may exceed expected data rates. In addition, in many cases, extra bandwidth needs to be allowed for the audio [42]. As with scaling, video compression can be subdivided into spatial (or intra-frame) and temporal (inter-frame) categories, which are both generally lossy in nature. Intra-frame compression typically employs either vector quantisation of groups of pixels or transform coding, where the pixels are transformed and then quantised (the latter is less computationally intensive and can be just as efficient) [23]. Discrete cosine transform is the most widely used method for transform coding of video [62]. Other options are wavelet compression and model-based compression. Inter-frame compression exploits areas of successive frames that do not change [23]. Of the many video codec standards [13], H.263, which is based on the earlier video-conferencing standard, H.261 [85, 29], is indicated and often used for low bit rate streaming applications [41, 84, 29, 71]. H.263 can withstand a reasonable amount of data loss, is recommended over unreliable networks and can be encoded in real time. However, there are restrictions over its permitted height and width [42]. Other codecs available for low bit rates include the evolving MPEG-4 standard [38, 26, 70] and the formats used with the proprietary architectures Apple QuickTime (including H.263 itself and Sorenson [26], which also has good quality for the Web [23]), RealNetworks (RealVideo 7, 8 and G2 proprietary formats [70]) [61] and Windows Media (Windows Media Video 7 or 8), the last of which is modelled on MPEG-4 [79, 70].

3.4   Packetisation

The Compressed Data Is Prepared for IP Transmission

Often performed by the compressing codec, another aspect to encoding streaming media data is packetisation, where the compressed data is prepared for IP transmission by wrapping it into IP packets. Streaming control information (metadata) may also be wrapped around the content [23].

3.5 Quality of Service Issues

Concerned With the Potential for Varying the Bit Rate

There are a number of performance issues, known as quality-of-service (QoS) issues, inherent in data networks that affect transmission of a video stream: bandwidth; delay, jitter and latency; and errors. A given network will not always be able to provide bandwidth guarantees [53]. Delay and jitter (due to errors in timing) can be reduced by buffering. Errors can result from network congestion, heavily delayed packets and general faults (data losses), which can all cause video artefacts. Depending on which video frames are affected, these can be of varying significance. More serious congestion and data loss can cause the transmission to be temporarily halted altogether [53]. Many networks do not have any control over QoS [53, 83], although there will be more support for this once IPv6 becomes more prevalent [23]. Tan and Zakhor state that two principal requirements for successful video transmission over the Internet are bandwidth adaptability and error resilience [77]. The former is concerned with the potential for varying the bit rate of the video depending on conditions in the network. These authors describe a TCP-friendly transmission scheme for video, which has the advantage of low latency and can satisfy the above requirements.

3.6 Video Architectures

The Compression of the Image Data

Streaming video architectures [26], also referred to as frameworks, multimedia subsystems [13] or streaming platforms [23] are essentially proprietary wrappers for video content, often together with information to help in decoding the inner file format [26]. The architecture essentially refers to the file format, which specifies the arrangement of the data in the file (including the image data), as opposed to the codec,

93

which describes the compression of the image data [42]. There are currently three main proprietary formats available on the market: QuickTime, RealNetworks and Windows Media [49, 27, 30]. All have their advantages and disadvantages, but unfortunately, unlike slower-to-market international standards, such as MPEG-4, interoperability between them leaves a great deal to be desired [13]. Also, none of the three is optimised for low bandwidth connections [39]:

• QuickTime: QuickTime was originally developed for Apple Macintosh computers and its player/encoder is shipped with every Mac operating system [49]. A free, basic player is available for Windows PCs and other platforms, and is easy to install; the streaming server software is also available free for most platforms [25]. Although QuickTime has been around for a long period of time, it came late to the streaming market, until recently only providing support for download-and-play and progressive download [79, 70]. The architecture continues to retain its popularity among Mac users [39], although its market penetrance outside this domain is relatively small compared with the other two main players [25].

• RealNetworks: Formerly ProgressiveNetworks, RealNetworks is a well established independent streaming solutions provider, which until recently had the greatest market penetrance [24, 49, 79, 65, 80], particularly in North America. However, as it does not sell operating systems, it is necessary for many of its products to be offered at a relatively high price, although the basic player is free [70]. The technology is compatible with various platforms. Although the player should be easy to install, it has been cited as frustratingly difficult and has an annoying nag screen for the paid version. The encoder is included with many editing tools [25], and content can be prepared for progressive download, which can be served from a conventional Web (HTTP) server [23].

RealVideo is highly scalable for different connection speeds [49, 65, 39] and has been reported to provide high quality video at low bit rates [80, 42]. It also has the option for encoding at multiple bit rates (SureStream) [79].

94

Unfortunately, its codecs, although of high quality and efficiency, are processor-intensive in terms of decoding, can only be played back on a Real client and it is not recommendable to convert from them [42].

- Windows Media: Microsoft's Windows Media is the newest of the three architectures and its player ships with current Windows PC operating systems [25]. It is therefore already overtaking RealNetworks in terms of market dominance [30], although RealNetworks claims a higher number of up-to-date users [70]. The Windows Media encoder is included with many editing tools [25], but its streaming server is only compatible with Windows servers [79], which, bearing in mind the dominance of Apache/Linux servers, is fairly limiting, although it is often provided as a free extra to NT servers [24]. Windows Media player has only recently been made available for Mac OS [25, 70] and is therefore rare among Mac users [65]. However, an advantage of this technology is that it supports encryption [25]. In addition, it is comparatively easy for novices to install and use [49].

- Java Players: Of the many other players available, Java applet players perhaps offer the most potential, as it is argued that they can run on any platform [60, 73, 40, 50], avoiding the need to have/download the latest player/update, a bugbear of many Web users [20, 49]. In theory, the required applet (which is low in file size) is downloaded automatically to the client machine when the user clicks the relevant link [49]. Java's pure implementation provides reasonable support for video or audio playback, albeit with a limited number of media formats [81], although its application programming interface (API), the Java Media Framework (JMF) [34, 46, 69], extends this to synchronised streaming of audio and video data over RTP [74, 51]. Various plug-ins are used to provide the necessary codecs for JMF [68, 19] and the technology runs on the Linux Apache server [68]. However, the latest version, 2.0, does not include method calls for receiving data across a network. An additional advantage of Java is that the technology is open-source, although there are licensing issues with some of the codecs, such as MPEG-4. The JMF is perhaps not as easy to use as claimed by Sun, requiring a great deal of programming expertise and understanding. A book to assist with this is recommended [74], although at the time of writing one was not available for version 2. Allison *et al.* provide a write up of JMF, although its disadvantages are not discussed [19]. Rohrig and Jochheim discuss the inconvenience of installing JMF libraries on the client's machine. In terms of communication between the applet and the server, VIC, a videoconferencing tool, has been used, with the IP address of the client being obtained via the server's common gateway interface (using a shell script) [68]. Mojsa and Zielinski used CORBA in their Java environment [60]. Fuentes and Troya used remote method invocation (RMI) to communicate between the client and the server, although the article does not provide much indication of the network they used [40]. Markousis *et al.* also used RMI, but the nature of the users (clients) is not specified [55]. Maly *et al.* describe a prototype distance learning system based on Java, using the JMF in conjunction with RTP and RTCP, although various issues remain unresolved, and the exact implementation and user installation are not described [54]. Li used a campus network for his study rather than the Internet [51]. Finally, Zhu and Georganas developed a videoconferencing application using JMF over a LAN, although again the end users are not mentioned [85].

3.7 Variable vs. Constant Bit Rate

The Option of Running Two Passes over the Data

Unless configured otherwise, codecs used for streaming encode at constant bit rates, which can result in a low quality of video during high action sequences [23]. Certain proprietary streaming codecs (in particular, RealVideo) therefore have the option of running two passes over the data to optimise the quality during encoding (which can impact on the file size), depending on the level of action [49, 79, 23]. Data passing through buffers on the server and player is then averaged [28].

96

Owing to the extra delay during encoding, this technique cannot be used with live content [23].

3.8 Multiple Bit Rates

Connection Speeds of One's Target Audience

Depending on the likely connection speeds of one's target audience, it was until recently necessary to prepare and provide more than one version of the content for different data rates [28, 33] using, for example, different levels of scaling and modes of compression. In some cases this is still the recommended way to do things [24]. The introduction of SureStream technology by RealNetworks (since the advent of the G2 codec in 1998) has allowed multiple bit rates to be encoded during pre-processing and stored in a given file [24, 79, 28]. Depending on network conditions and the speed of connection, the server can then switch between streams accordingly [28]. Unfortunately, the technology is only available for use with streaming servers (ie, not with traditional Web servers and progressive download) [66] and is not always recommended [24]. By using Intel's Indeo 5 codec, Ligos has also developed a product, which encodes at multiple bit rates, so that a viewer with a low speed connection can view a degraded quality file while a premium quality version is being downloaded simultaneously. However, the downside of this is that the quality of the preview could be very low and it could take considerably longer for the high quality file to be downloaded [33].

3.9 Copyright Protection

Conditional Access Is Concerned With Providing a Licence

Maintaining intellectual property and obtaining revenue/preventing financial loss are important considerations for the multimedia content developer/provider, resulting in considerable research on the subject. As the Internet has public access, Austerberry (2002) defines the two main goals of digital rights management as maintaining confidentiality and providing restricted access to entertainment [23]. Lin *et al.* describe the main issues of copyright control as concerning conditional access, authentication, copy control/protection and content tracking [52]. In the case of streaming media, the bit stream needs to be protected from unauthorised access, which might result in tampering [64], copying and supply [52] that would provide gain or a challenge for pirates and hackers [23]. Conditional access is concerned with providing a licence (often subject to a fee), which allows the user to access the material, in some cases a restricted number of times. This may be enforced by the use of cryptography, so that a decryption key is necessary for the user to access the content [52]. Keys can be either symmetric (shared secret) or asymmetric (public/private key) and can be delivered in a variety of ways [23]. In addition to providing authentication (verification of identity) of both the source and the receiver, and authorisation certificates [37, 23], cryptography can be employed to encrypt content (this is usually the first line of defence). For streaming applications, encryption must take place at the packet level to enable the viewer to view the content in real time. However, often more than one system is required if more than one architecture is provided [23]. Encryption of streaming media can take place prior to storage or on the fly [37, 23]. Wolfgang *et al.* believe that encrypted digital content is of limited use because the media becomes unviewable. The same authors cite time stamping, where the owner of the media file can be ascertained from the earliest time stamp, as "critical to the success of any multimedia security system" [82]. Copy control is involved with the protection against unauthorised copying of material and often employs the use of watermarking technology (comprehensive reviews are provided on this subject [82, 43, 52]). Overtly visible watermarks tend to be employed for preview copies [23], while invisible digital watermarks, also known as perceptual watermarks [82], are used for high quality content, and can be tracked using Web spiders [23]. Digital watermarks should be robust against attack and data conversion/manipulation, imperceptible and informative, while their embedding and retrieval should be fairly straightforward, including in real-time situations [43]. Watermarking of digital video is challenging as the stored and transmitted content is often compressed [43], the watermarks can be damaged as a result of errors in the transmission network [52] and because attackers could deduce a watermark from a comparison of different frames [82]. Audio content can also be watermarked, which is particularly challenging as a result of the sensitivity of the human audible system and the lower sampling rates of data in which to embed information [43]. Hartung and Kutter's review cites several techniques which have been used successfully to embed watermarks in audio content. 'Man in the middle' attacks from the network (where hackers can spoof an individual's identity) can also be a threat to security, as can the clients themselves. No mechanism is 100 per cent failsafe and the cost of security provision has to be weighed up against the risk for and consequence of any loss, together with the additional consideration of enabling straightforward access. There are a variety of models available for deriving financial benefit from content online [23].

3.10 Multimedia Content on Web Sites

The Inclusion of Multimedia Content on Web Sites

The benefits that can be gained from the inclusion of multimedia content on Web sites, particularly for educational purposes, are well documented. However, the successful use of real-time applications over networks has, in the past, been hindered by limitations in the technology and the infrastructure used; notably, the compression algorithms and transmission protocols available, and the bandwidth of the connections concerned (many users access the Internet via dial-up modems). Furthermore, real-time transmissions have their own quality of service issues. As a method of data transfer, download-and-play is not ideal for multimedia content, as the excessive delay often experienced tends to frustrate the user. In contrast, both true streaming and progressive download mechanisms have their own significant benefits, depending on, for example, the type of content, the intended audience and the available budget. There is a wide variety of compression algorithms available for video and audio content, which are improving all the time, together with emerging standards, such as MPEG-4. Apple QuickTime RealNetworks and Windows Media are the three major proprietary architectures currently available for streaming multimedia, again, each with its own advantages and disadvantages. Offering great promise are Java applet players that are platform-independent, since despite their market penetration, proprietary architectures lack interoperability. However, it currently appears to be difficult to stream synchronised content using Java's API, JMF, across the Internet. Other promising technologies include variable bit rate encoding and opportunities to encode at multiple bit rates.

Protecting rights to and maximising financial return from digital content are important considerations for the content developer/provider, although no mechanism of protection is 100 per cent failsafe and the associated cost and ease of use should be kept in perspective. Encryption and watermarking technologies are widely used, the former often being employed for authentication purposes and the latter for tracking usage. The author concludes that the addition of multimedia content to an artist's Web site for the purposes of demonstrating a technique would be a worthwhile undertaking. In terms of implementation, the logistics of the various options available would need to consider from a practical perspective in order to determine the best approach.

3.11 Independently of Any Bureaucracy

Fear or Apprehension Surrounding the Use of Digital Technology

Prior to 1994, the art world was in a state of recovery following the recession of the 1980s, so had not yet colonised the Internet. Its use flourished throughout the latter half of the 1990s. Net artists' exploit the characteristics peculiar to the medium, such as immediacy and immateriality. The Internet has enabled practitioners to communicate on equal ground, across international boundaries, instantaneously, every day and to work and talk independently of any bureaucracy or art-world institution without being marginalised or deprived of community.

Some artists chose to go digital or to stay traditional or experiment somewhere in between. There are those artists using traditional media who have not yet recognised the possibilities of digital technology as a valuable tool or who have chosen not to explore the possibilities based on subjective bias [2]. The fear or apprehension surrounding the use of digital technology within the fine arts may be associated with preconceptions that it is more appropriate to commercial applications and, in particular, graphic design. The physicality of traditional media can appear incongruous with the use of digital technology. However, technological developments in recent years have greatly increased the number of options available to visual artists for conceiving and creating art works.

Back in 1987, the German engineering company Fraunhofer IIS designed a standard for digitally storing audio files with near CD-quality sound, MP3 (short for MPEG Audio Layer 3). The advent of MP3 was perhaps the most important development in the ease of digital storage and transfer of musical recording. The technique has been central to a revolution affecting every aspect of the music industry. With the file size of a digital version of a piece of music reduced, all that was needed was an easy transfer service and it came in the form of Napster, the Net phenomenon that shocked the music industry.

At present, the legitimate music sites only offer music from a couple of record labels at most, making it hard to find exactly what you are looking for within the same site. Customers may waste hours surfing the Web to find what they want, if the legitimate download even exists at all. Customers want the right to control their music the way they want, which means the right to copy music onto a CD or MP3 player without the fear of breaking copyright laws [3].

3.12 Riginal Print

Hallmarks of an Original Print

With the advent of techniques capable of photomechanically reproducing an artist's work in the 1890s, it soon became necessary for the buyer to be able to distinguish between an original print and a reproduction. However, formal or legal definitions did not appear until the 1960s, during which time the Third International Congress of Artists in Vienna (in 1960) devised a definition that was to fuel many others later used in a number of countries.

When used as a noun, original refers specifically to a print . . . every single copy of a woodcut etching or lithograph is an "original," the final and complete embodiment of the artist's intention. The miracle of the process is that there are not one but many originals. The four main printmaking media are etching, lithography, screen-printing and relief printing. However, an original print is made when the artist creates a new piece of work by working with one (or more) of the printmaking media. This is "unlike a reproduction, where an original painting is photographed and then mechanically printed en-mass resulting in what is essentially a poster, not an original print" [4]. If a set of original prints is identical, they are considered a limited edition, one of the hallmarks of an original print (as is the artist's signature). The prints are carefully printed and numbered by hand, signed by the artist and then the original plate(s) should be destroyed. The entire process therefore involves artistic input from creation to completion to produce a print that will sell at a fraction of the cost of an original painting or drawing.

In 1961, the Print Council of America [5], issued the following criteria for identifying an original print (the Council currently acknowledges that such a definition is now difficult):

- The artist alone must create the master image on the original material

- The print should be hand printed by the artist or someone under his or her supervision

- Each print should be approved and signed by the artist and the master image destroyed or cancelled

- The original print should not be a copy of any other image unless produced in another medium by the same artist previously.

An original print cannot be defined or assessed solely in terms of the technique or process used. Therefore an original print work should be conceived by the artist for a graphic process in order to widen the distribution of an original idea. The fact is that the limited edition number and the signature, the extraneous factors often looked for on an original print, are the easiest items to add to a photomechanical reproduction, thereby creating the misleading impression that it is, in fact, an original print. To include each successive impression created through contact with an inked or un-inked stone, block, plate or screen that was worked upon by the artist alone or with others; it may be directly controlled or supervised by the artist and must meet his criteria for excellence. The International Fine Print Dealers Association considers that the term "originality" used in the above context has become bankrupt and imprecise and specifies new standards based on a rather complicated numerical scheme, which it claims will remain valid for years to come.

The overriding message from much of the literature is that artists' and dealers' main motives for establishing a Web presence is to make the art and music available to a much wider, international audience. The Web has opened up the British and Asian art market to a wider audience. Art sites can serve as a starting point for beginners who want to learn about art but who might otherwise feel intimidated about art galleries, enabling them to get an idea about prices and future exhibitions. Sites also allow experienced collectors the opportunity to view works via the Internet when they might otherwise be pushed for time. Web is no substitute for the real thing, particularly for the inexperienced buyer. Although much hyped, the recently emerging thought is that [6] "pure Internet art dealerships" do not offer the personal service of the traditional art trade and encouragement to develop an understanding and appreciation of "difficult" pictures.

The multimedia capabilities of the Internet have provided major appeal for some artists wanting to present video or sound clips of their work. Freely available software allows compressed video and audio to be streamed on most computers without download delays. The increased use of streamed sound and video as well as remote interaction are transforming the level of Web-based interaction. The evolving environment of the Web provides a unique challenge for artists to explore these conjunctions of cyberspace, media and audience feedback. While on the one hand shrinkage of royalty payments threatened traditional artists and the musicians signed up with the record companies, the incredible distribution network offered by the Net has helped launch others who may have not received openings into the market. It could be argued that in this way the Net is resulting in an expansion of the market. But the future is not all rosy, and there remains much that needs to be done in order to make the Internet a widely acceptable marketplace for the exchange of goods and services between merchants and consumers. Technology continues to become more complex and the safeguards used today may be severely out of date tomorrow.

3.13 Concern for the Music Industry

Legitimate or Illegitimate Sound Recording

Since the late 1990s the explosion in file sharing on the Net has escalated music piracy to astonishing levels. Legitimate or illegitimate sound recording can be electronically transported around the world and downloaded directly into computer hard drives and copied onto CD-R disc. The pirate music market has never been more appealing and simpler to the consumer. Illegally downloaded music on the Internet is deemed to be at crisis point, forcing the industry to continually throw millions of pounds at campaigns aimed at eradicating the problem.

Within the Internet culture of unlicensed use, theft of intellectual property is rampant and has given music pirates a new weapon. Piracy affects every sector of the music industry from retailers to distributors, artists, composers, publishers, record companies and ultimately the consumer. Illegal Internet file-sharing services most commonly using Peer-2-Peer networks have taken the lead in forming an electronic marketplace, giving music consumers exactly what they want, when they want, and at a price they want it – free! Music can be downloaded without authorisation or compensation to the artist. Other music pirates use the Internet as a tool to peddle illegal CDs.

Furthermore, freed from the potential constraints dictated by major record labels as well as the physical limitations imposed by making and distributing a CD, artists can take advantage of options previously unfeasible. For example, different versions of the same song can easily be made available to the public via MP3 files. Other advantages of the music-on-the-Internet experience include the ability to link complementary information never found in liner notes, such as scoring arrangements. At lenistern.com not only can fans listen to music, they can make credit cards purchases of hard copies of Stern's CDs as well as online downloads of individual tracks. This direct method of distribution that cuts out the need for the large record company is increasingly appealing to artists. The largest benefit of online music technology, for both musicians and consumers alike, is getting the music out there. In addition to individual sites such as LSR, several small companies specialise in providing music in MP3 files, including MP3.com and Mjuice.com. The current legal questions about peer-to-peer programs leave the future of music and the Internet open to huge speculation. One of the most significant issues for Napster and related systems is that the music is free. Listeners wanting to search for particular songs can download the MP3 files directly from another person. So not only will the big five record companies lose out on the money, so will independent labels. The seduction of peer-to-peer systems – sharing massive amounts of material – is also one of the biggest drawbacks. The potential of sharing unwanted material, such as viruses, could still persuade listeners to seek out their tunes from central sources, such as LSR's Website or MP3.com [7].

The global pirate music market totalled 1.9 billion units in 2001. Discs make up the majority of pirate sales overtaking cassettes for the first time, and reflect the switch in piracy to recordable CDs (CD-R) discs. The International Federation of Phonographic Industry (IFPI) estimates that 28 percent of all CDs sold in 2001 were pirate. The total is split roughly evenly between CD audio discs made on factory production lines and those made in smaller scale CD-R operations in garages and labs. Worldwide sales of pressed pirate CDs were 500 million units, up from 475 million in 2000, with pirate CD-R discs estimated at around 450 million units, up from 165 million in 2000 [8]. The major trend in music piracy around the world is the growth in CD-R demand. Using the UK market as an example, CD-R demand in 2001 has seen 308m blank recordable CDs sold. Independent sources estimate that 128m of these were used to record music [9].

The low cost of Internet art and music compared with conventional CD catalogues is another factor involved in the placement of art and music on the Web. A report on the virtual Internet gallery [10], states that the Web is particularly useful for exhibiting art, as visualisation is the most important consideration, whereas the physical presence of the object exhibited is only of secondary concern. The existing art sites are merely electronic versions of conventional printed catalogues and that they "do not take further advantage of the new media." Limitations in the existing technology include unreliable colour on displays, limited display area and loss of canvas structure. However, there are cultural opportunities in that artists and potential buyers can communicate irrespective of temporal and spatial limitations. The Internet provides artists with more control over how their work is represented than conventional printed catalogues and relieves the pressure of recouping expenses.

3.14 Low Cost of Disseminating Work to a Wide Audience

Concerned with Marketing

The low cost of disseminating work to a wide audience via the Web creates a distinction between the terms "*art on the Net*" and the rarer "*Net art*". One is concerned with marketing, and possibly selling, conventional work via the Web. The other is the art in itself that takes advantage of the medium in its creation and distribution. These areas overlap somewhat. The Web can empower unknown artists, who are able to bypass art galleries. However, galleries, although sometimes biased and conservative, have a role in filtering out the rubbish, so the result is a great deal of artistic incompetence available online [11]. The other danger is that just because something is online does not make it radical or attractive. Art dealers are in agreement that the Web radically increases international exposure and that the medium offers a promotional opportunity that they would be unwise to ignore. Although sales of original paintings on the Internet have been disappointing (customers like to see the work in person), sales of original prints have been more promising.

It is perfectly legal for consumers to copy music for their own enjoyment, i.e., non-commercial use. Congress has even declared, in the Audio Home Recording Act of 1992, that it is legal to make recordings and lend them to people, provided it is not done for commercial purposes. According to SoundScan (the system, introduced in 1991, that measures album purchases at their point of sale, giving the industry precise sales figures), it is unlawful, of course, if it's done to make a profit. For an industry that's been able to bank on year-to-year sales increases, business through the first six months of 2002 was down 5.4 percent. Just look at how many copies, combined, the top 10 sellers in year 2001 have sold: 22 million. Now compare that with the combined sales for the biggest 10 hits of July 2000: 36 million. The big music chains are feeling that sluggishness as well, which explains why venerable CD seller Tower records, with nearly 200 stores worldwide, is battling creditors to avoid a bankruptcy filing. The company posted $34 million in losses during the first quarter in 2001. Like all the major music retailers, Tower has been hurt by disappointing sales as well as stiff competition from mass-market retailers like Best Buy and Target, which sell CDs on the cheap in order to build foot traffic. In the wake of the Napster debate, an argument could be made that savvy consumers are simply no longer doling out cash for CDs. They're still devouring new music at a healthy rate, swapping files with friends, but it's just not showing up in SoundScan [12]. Most artists, who traditionally depend upon the large record companies, obviously stand to lose royalty payments with the dissolution of distribution through the Net. Interestingly, however, there are examples of artists who are taking advantage of the changing scenario.

Leni Stern, jazz guitarist/singer/songwriter, is a case in point where online technology has meant greater artistic control as well as more immediate contact with her fans. Stern, who began her music career in 1977, started her own record label, Leni Stern Recordings (LSR) in 1997 with the idea of promoting herself and, subsequently, other recording artists as well. Having her own label provides Stern the freedom to work according to her own schedule while controlling her production. MP3 technology and the Internet allow Stern to bypass the traditional recording industry format – a complete CD of songs – and offer visitors to her Website the chance to listen to new music before it is released in stores. Visitors can also access music that is available exclusively on the Internet. The digital technology has enabled a wide range of converging technologies, such as video, audio and the Internet, to unite so that the spectator is actively engaged outside the gallery context. This has led to new audiences, although there is a growing suspicion that such multimedia art represents technology-led research and often fails to work or is over-hyped [13]. Despite the increased audience for many art and music sites, there are concerns for Internet traffic to a given site. Income and computer literacy characterise the virtual public inhabiting cyberspace. It is less inclusive than the public encountering other projects in the streets. An imbalance between content and its display will 'leave a viewer unfulfilled. Similarly, there are dangers of overlooking the content on sites while getting the flashy animations to work.

Furthermore, art collecting via the Web is more wishful thinking than reality. It is a viable art mechanism with particularly distinct characteristics. The inherent characteristics of Web-based communication can be exploited to extend the gallery metaphor, taking advantage of the absence of discrete boundaries, idiosyncrasies of transmission of information and an interface-driven environment. Part of the appeal of placing art on the Web relates to the scope for interaction and feedback from a viewer base that would not otherwise be feasible, given the narrow cast nature of much of the contemporary art circles [14]. Web-based interactions are further transformed by the increasing employment of streaming sound and video and remote interaction as a result of tremendous progress in video compression and transmission. The use of digital video in multimedia systems and over the Internet is becoming pervasive.

The Internet revolution, rise of digital technology, and the newness of bandwidth connections have raised a number of challenges for the traditional art painting and music industry. The huge popularity of the music file sharing services like Napster sent shock waves through the industry. Closer examination suggests, however, that technological and consumption pattern changes do not necessarily spell the end of profitability. Similar fears were voiced about the movie industry following the popularity of cable and home video, but the cinema audience has only grown. In a sense the new technologies only served to expand and multiply demand for movies. The success of traditional artists and musicians willing to be creative with the marketing opportunities offered by the world of the new media proves that it is possible to use the new media to boost old media success. The risks involved cannot be measured in terms of financial losses.

Ultimately, the music industry's war on illegal downloading can never be won. In the future legitimate music services will flourish, but only because they will eventually sufficiently cater for the consumer market. Previously illegal services, ideologies and technology will be adapted and incorporated in the future services on the music industry. The only pitfall for the industry is incurring the wrath of the consumers by labelling them as criminals and invading their privacy rights. With a consumer movement of the magnitude witnessed by Peer-2-Peer file sharing services, the industry must take note that the services it provides are insufficient and not just blame illegal downloading for all of its problems.

It is obvious from the data presented that illegal downloading is huge among the consumer but it is debatable whether CD sales are affected by illegal downloading or if illegal services actually encourage the use of legitimate services. A survey conducted by Forrester on 1000 online consumers suggests that digital music doesn't effect their illegitimate purchasing of CDs and the main problem is the economy and competition from the games industry [3]. It could be that the mass hysteria of the industry is ultimately a ploy to implement undesirable laws and regulations on the pirates and consumers. Most paramount to future development of legitimate online services is how the industry will make the experience of buying digital music more appealing to customers whilst attracting them away from the illegal services.

3.15 Conclusion

Wide Variances of Interpretation and Execution

In an examination of the implications of experiencing art works through the Internet, technologies [15] such as Java allow users to "respond more actively and spontaneously" to vivid and communicative art sites compared with conventional HTML pages. Artists have made use of the Web in various ways: some have used it to present information about themselves and their work in other media while others have been drawn to this interface by its relevance to the logic of their own artistic development. Many artists have made critical presentations that attempt to reveal the parameters of computer-mediated communications and the potential for representing pre-existing material, the online textual, visual, multimedia mix (collage) and the hybrid use of images, text, sound and video. In order to address the risk of unauthorised use of material over the Net, we can refer to existing IPR law and associated remedies for breach of copyright and patent protection. First, copyright law does apply to materials on Web sites. This is the case even if the author does not mind his/her work being freely available to anyone. As in the instance of false claim of ownership, the true originator would understandably want to exercise his/her rights under copyright law – abandonment of economic protection does not mean an equal waiver of moral rights [16]. Piracy has always been a major concern for the music industry and can range from individuals making several replicas of legitimate CDs and tapes to the millions sold to help fund criminal or even terrorist activity of organised gangs. In territories such as China, Russia, Brazil and Mexico piracy levels are so high it is exceptionally difficult to develop a legitimate market for recorded music. The music industry loses more than $1 billion per year from illegal activities conducted in these countries, not including losses due to Internet piracy [8].

In 1999, Crowley reported that the technology associated with streaming media was inadequate for mainstream use and that the cost could be prohibitive. She therefore advised that it should be reserved for use only where it was absolutely necessary [31]. However, significant advances have been made since that time and the use of broadband technology is continuing to gain popularity.

The rich media has proved to be useful in the past for distance learning, news feeds and corporate product launches, and can also be used for music promotion [23]. Alvear states that training is the 'killer application' for enterprise video as a result of convenience, cost, better self-pacing and learning retention [20]. In the future, the options for streaming media will be improved by the increased availability of better compression algorithms and high bandwidth connections. However, a consequence of the latter may be that bottlenecks in performance could move closer to the server, which to some extent is already occurring [80]. Other improvements may result from better use of satellite distribution to avoid congested parts of the Internet, new and improved protocols, CDNs, multicasting technology (avoiding duplication), convergence of TV and IP to widen accessibility, and more interoperability and better standards, such as MPEG-4 [20, 23] (which is highly scalable and provides acceptable quality over dial-up connections [42]). Another possibility is that Java will come into its own as it will be supported by set-top boxes and 3rd generation mobile communications, whereas the current players are not (D. Austerberry, personal communication).

The Internet is a source of education, pleasure and open discussion. So the question remains, *how can original art and music be safeguarded?* The conclusion is that there is no need for a single, global Internet regulator. The generic nature of any proposed body would hinder some countries, while allowing others perhaps too much freedom. Also, the regulations put forward would be open to wide variances of interpretation and execution. The better approach would be to facilitate the coming together of the necessary bodies to ensure there are no contradictions or major exposures that could harm the progress of multimedia-enriched Web sites. Based on our research and personal opinion, multimedia technologies are here to stay. Nevertheless, many questions concerning technology remain unanswered and frequently unasked [18].

References

1   Power, R (2002), *Tangled Web,* Que Corporation.

2   Labadie, J. A. (2001) The graphical interface in the digital millennium: the past is present. Proceedings of the Fifth *International Conference on Information Visualisation.* pp245-247

3   Bernoff, J (2002), "Downloads Save the Music Business," http://www.forrester.com/ER/Research/Report/Summary/0,1338,14854,00.h tml, (Accessed 28 October 2002).

4   Zigrosser, C. (1956) The Book of Fine Prints. New York, Crown

5   Print Council of America (1961) What is an Original Print?: Principles Recommended by the *Print Council of America,* Edited by Joshua Binion Cahn. *Print Council of America (2000),* Defining a print. www.printcouncil.org/defining_a_print.html, (Accessed 3 Jan 2003).

6   Flynn, T. (2001) E-phemeral mail, *ArtReview,* p 69, June.

7   Sun Microsystems' "Digital Journey" (2001), Digital Downloads: MP3 and Beyond. www.sun.com (Accessed 12 Dec 2002)

8   Music Piracy Report 2002 (2002), *The International Federation of the Phonographic Industry* (IFPI), p 1-10, June.

9   Piracy Report 2001 (2002), British Phonographic Industry (BPI), p 1-4, June.

10 Müller, A., Leissler, M., Hemmje, M. & Neuhold, E. (1999) Towards the Virtual Internet gallery. *IEEE International Conference on Multimedia Computing and Systems,* Volume 2, pp 214-219

11 Whittaker, D. (1997) Networks. ArtReview, p 7, October.

12 Eric Boehlert (2001), What's wrong with the music biz?, July. www.salon.com, (Accessed 8 Nov 2002).

13 Ashbee, B. (2000) Don't just lie there – interact! *ArtReview,* pp 56-59, June.

14 Weintraub. A. (1997) Art on the Web, *Communications of the ACM,* 97-102, October.

15 Oh, J.K., and Lim, G.C., (1997) Problems and possibilities of the experience of modern art through the Internet, Proceedings of INET97.

16 Bainbridge, D.I., (2000), (Barrister Aston Business School), "Intellectual Property", Financial Times Pitman.

17   Dutton W.H., (1999), Society On the Line, Information Politics in the Digital Age, Pub Oxford.

18   Dr Preston, D. S., (2001), Technology, Managerialism, and the University, Glenrothes.

19   Allison, C., Bateman, M. & Ruddle, A. (2001) Realising real time multimedia groupware on the web. *Proceedings of the IEEE Multimedia Workshop*, Manchester, 8 September

20   Alvear, J. (1998) *Guide to Streaming Multimedia*. New York: Wiley Computer Publishing

21   Apteker, R. T., Fisher, J. A., Kisimov, V. S. & Neishlos, H. (1995) Video acceptability and frame rate. *IEEE Multimedia* 2(3), pp32-40

22   Ashour, G., Amir, A., Ponceleon, D. & Srinivasan, S. (2000) Architecture for varying multimedia formats. *Proceedings of the 2000 ACM Multimedia Workshop*, Marina Del Rey, November. pp85-88

23   Austerberry, D. (2002) *The Technology of Video & Audio Streaming*. Oxford: Focal Press

24   Bagwell, C. (2000) Multimedia on the Internet: Streaming Media West '99. *Library Hi Tech News* 17(4), pp1-5

25   Bell, E. & Bell, H. (2001) Special delivery. *Electronic Musician* 17(9), p74

26   Bloodworth, C. (2001) Video architectures and codecs. *Videomaker* 15(10), p50

27   Civanlar, M. R., Luthra, A., Wenger, S. & Zhu, W. (2001) Introduction to the special issue on streaming video. *IEEE Transactions on Circuits and Systems for Video Technology* 11(3), pp265-268

28   Conklin, G. J., Greenbaum, G. S., Lillevold, K. O., Lippman, A. F. & Reznik, Y. A. (2001) Video coding for streaming media delivery on the Internet. *IEEE Transactions on Circuits and Systems for Video Technology* 11(3), pp269-281

29   Côté, G., Erol, B. Gallant, M. & Kossentini, F. (1998) H.263+: video coding at low bit rates. *IEEE Transactions on Circuits and Systems for Video Technology* 8(7), pp849-866

30   Covell, A. (2001) Reel 'Em IN! *Network Computing*, 19 February, p46

31   Crowley, A. (1999) Is Web multimedia ready for mainstream? *PC Week* 16(5), 1 February, p69

32   Dajen (2002) Streaming [Online] Available at www.dajen.com/video_ streaming.html (accessed 22 October 2002)

33   Davis, J. L. (2001) Serverless streaming. *Videomaker* 15(10), p71

34   deCarmo, (1998) The ultimate multimedia Lego set. *PC Magazine* 17(6), 24 March, pp256-258

35   Destounis, P., Garofalakis, J., Kappos, P. & Tzimas, J. (2001) Measuring the mean Web page size and its compression to limit latency and improve download time. *Internet Research: Electronic Networking Applications and Policy* 11(1), pp10-17

36   Dipert, B. (2002) *EDN* hands-on story: video characterization creates hands-on headaches. *EDN* 47(6), 25 July, pp53-58

37   Editvu-SECURITY (2002) Your content is well-protected [Online] Available at www.editvu.com/security.html

38   Fernando, G. (2000) MPEG-4 makes the grade as a net-centric standard. *Electronic Engineering Times*, 13 November, p124

39   Fong, A. C. M. & Hui, S. C. (2002) An end-to-end solution for Internet lecture delivery. *Campus-Wide Information Systems* 19(2), pp45-51

40   Fuentes, L. & Troya, J. M. (1999) A Java framework for Web-based multimedia and collaborative applications. *IEEE Internet Computing*, March-April, pp55-64

41   Gemmell, D. J. & Bell, C. G. (1997) Noncollaborative telepresentations come of age. *Communications of the ACM* 40(4), pp79-89

42   Gulie, S. (2002) *QuickTime for the Web: for Windows and Macintosh*, 2nd edn. San Francisco: Morgan Kaufmann

43   Hartung, F. & Kutter, M. (1999) Multimedia watermarking techniques. *Proceedings of the IEEE* 87(7), pp1079-1107

44   Hashmi, M. A. & Guvenli, T. (2001) Multimedia content on the Web: problems and prospects. *Managerial Finance* 27(7), pp34-41

45   Hickok, J. (2002) Web library tours: using streaming video and interactive quizzes. *Reference Services Review* 30(2), pp99-111

46   IBM (1999) An introduction to the Java Media Framework Application Programming Interface [Online] Available at www-106.ibm.com/developerworks/library/jmf/jmfwhite.html

47   Kim, B. C. & Severance, C. (1999) Multi-media enhancement of teaching electronic packaging education. *Proceedings of the 49th Electronic Components and Technology Conference*, San Diego, 1-4 June, pp904-906

48   Knee, R., Musgrove, A. & Musgrove, J. (2000) Lights, camera, action! *Learning & Leading with Technology* 28(1), September, p50

49   Lawton, G. (2000) Video streams into the mainstream. *IEEE Computer*, July, pp12-17

50   Lee, D. Y., Ji, C. H., Ha, H. K., Jeong, S. G., Keh, J. E., Choi, K. K., Kim, C. D. & Lee, M. H. (2001) 3-D position analysis of an object using a monocular USB port camera through Java. *Proceedings of the IEEE International Symposium on Industrial Electronics*, Pusan, South Korea, 12-16 June, pp2028-2032

51   Li, S.-T. (2002) A platform-neutral live IP/TV presentation system. *Information Sciences* 140, pp33-52

52   Lin, E. T., Cook, G. W., Salama, P. & Delp, E. J. (2001a) An overview of security issues in streaming video. *Proceedings of the International Conference on Information Technology: Coding and Computing*, Las Vegas, 2-4 April, pp345-348

53   Lin, E. T., Podilchuk, C. I., Kalker, T. & Delp, E. J. (2001b) Streaming video and rate scalable compression: what are the challenges for watermarking. *Proceedings of the SPIE, The International Society for Optical Engineering*, Sane Jose, January, pp116-127

54   Maly, K., Abdel-Wahab, H., Wild, C., Overstreet, C. M., Gupta, A., Abdel-Hamid, A., Ghanem, S., Gonzalez, A. & Zhu, X. (2001) IRI-h, a Java-based distance education system: architecture and performance. *ACM Journal of Educational Resources in Computing*, 1, Spring, pp1-15

55   Markousis, Th., Tsirikos, D., Vazirgiannis, M. & Stavrakas, Y. (2000) WWW-enabled delivery of interactive multimedia documents. *Computer Communications* 23, pp242-252

56   Masry, M. & Hemami, S. S. (2001) An analysis of subjective quality in low bit rate video. *Proceedings of the 2001 International Conference on Image Processing* 1, pp465-468

57   McCormack, C. & Jones, D. (1998) *Building a Web-based Education System*. New York: Wiley

58   MCH Netlink Plus (2002) Media streaming. The process – an overview [Online] Available at mchnetlinkplus.ichp.edu/MediaStreaming/Process.htm (accessed 22 October 2002)

59   Medianet (2002) Progressive download vs streaming: the facts [Online] Available at www.medianet-usa.com/progressive.html (accessed 22 October 2002)

60   Mojsa, T. & Zielinski, K. (1997) Web enabled, CORBA driven, distributed videotalk environment on the Java platform. *Computer Networks and ISDN Systems* 29, pp865-873

61   Mungee, S., Surendran, N. & Schmidt, D. C. (1999) The design and performance of a CORBA audio/video streaming service. *Proceedings of the 32nd Hawaii International Conference on System Sciences* Maui, Hawaii, 5-8 January, pp1-18

62   Pao, I.-M. & Sun, M.-T. (2001) Encoding stored video for streaming applications. *IEEE Transactions on Circuits and Systems for Video Technology* 11(2), pp199-209

63   Popwire Technology [Online] Available at www.popwire.com/glossary3e.htm (accessed 22 October 2002)

64   Rees, J. (1994) Information access versus document supply. The
      International Visual Arts Information Network Project. *Interlending and
      Document Supply* 22(1), pp20-24

65   Reid, D. (2001) Compressing video for the future: video compression for
      non-broadcast delivery. *Advanced Imaging* 16(5), p49

66   Roback, S. (1999) Islands in the stream. *AV Video Multimedia Producer*
      21(12), p108

67   Rodriguez, A. A. & Morse, K. (1994) Evaluating video codecs. *IEEE
      Multimedia* 1(3), Autumn, pp25-33

68   Rohrig, C. & Jochheim, A. (1999) The virtual lab for controlling real
      experiments via Internet. *Proceedings of the IEEE Conference on Computer
      Aided Control System Design*, Kohala Coast, Hawaii, 22-27 August, pp279-
      284

69   Sales, M. (1999) Java Media Framework supports array of format roles.
      Electronic Engineering Times, 22 November, p74

70   Sauer, J. (2001) The stream team: a digital video format primer. *EMedia
      Magazine* 14(10), October, pp36-41

71   Servetto, S. D. & Nahrstedt, K. (1999) Video streaming over the public
      internet: multiple description codes and adaptive transport protocols.
      Proceedings of the International Conference on Image Processing, 3, Kobe,
      24-28 October, pp85-89

72   Shapiro, M. (1999) Shoot for the web. *Camcorder & Computer Video*
      15(11), p84

73   Shin, M.-K. & Lee, J.-Y. (1998) A web-based real-time multimedia
      application for the MBone. *Proceedings of the INET'98 Conference*,
      Geneva, 21-24 July

74   Simpson-Young, B. (1999) Reviews. Programming with the Java Media
      Framework. *Internet Research: Electronic Networking Applications and
      Policy* 9(2), p41

75   Sorenson Media. Compression [Online] Available at www.sorenson.com/
      content.php?cats=3/12/69 (accessed 22 October 2002)

76   Talagala, N., Asami, S. & Patterson, D. (1999) Usage patterns of a Web-
      based image collection. *Proceedings of the 16th IEEE Symposium on Mass
      Storage Systems*, San Diego, 15-18 March, pp203-214

77   Tan, W. & Zakhor, A. (1999) Real-time Internet video using error resilient
      scalable compression and TCP-friendly transport protocol. *IEEE
      Transactions on Multimedia* 1, pp172-186

78   Turpentyne Productions. Digital video and audio [Online] Available at
      www.turpentyneproductions.com/digital.htm (accessed 22 October 2002)

79   Waggoner, B. (2000) Choosing a streaming video technology. *DV Web
      Video* [Online] Available at
      http://www.dvwebvideo.com/2000/0500/waggoner0500.html

80   Wang, Y., Claypool, M. & Zuo, Z. (2001) An empirical study of RealVideo performance across the Internet. *Proceedings of the First ACM SIGCOMM Internet Measurement Workshop*, San Francisco, 1-2 November

81   WebWorkshop [Online] Available at http://www.ictp.trieste.it/~its/1999/webworkshop/lectures/douglas/media/mediamain.html (accessed 17 November 2002)

82   Wolfgang, R. B., Podilchuk, C. I. & Delp, E. J. (1999) Perceptual watermarks for digital images and video. *Proceedings of the IEEE* 87(7), pp1108-1126

83   Wu, D., Hou, Y. T., Zhu, W., Zhang, Y.-Q. & Peha, J. M. (2001) Streaming video over the Internet: approaches and directions. *IEEE Transactions on Circuits and Systems for Video Technology* 11(3), pp282-300

84   Zhu, C. RTP payload format for H.263 video streams. RFC 2190 [Online] Available at www.faqs.org/rfcs/rfc2190.html (accessed 18 September 2002)

85   Zhu, W. & Georganas, N. D. (2001) JQOS: a QoS-based internet videoconferencing system using the Java Media Framework (JMF). *Canadian Conference on Electrical and Computer Engineering* 1, Toronto, 13-16 May, pp625-630

4

Patentability: Questions About the Control of Strategic Technology

4.1 Introduction

This chapter looks at the extension of patentability to new subject matter in Europe and The United States: questions about the control of strategic technology. Whereas industrial property right was born in the 16th century in Italy and then, in the course of the following centuries, spread through industrial countries, today's new standards of patentability are coming from the US. New scientific and technical fields were opened to patents, notably biotechnology and Information and communication technology, with their key products: genetic and software inventions. In Europe, the adaptation of the legal framework is subject to many debates, and its fragmentation hinders European competitiveness and the catching up with the US level of development. However, is it worth adapting the European regime of industrial property on the US model? On the one hand, such an adaptation questions the real role of patent (is it really an incentive to innovate?). On the other hand, is this unified legal framework not going to reinforce the gap between countries which will be able to patent and those which will not be able to?

4.2 Inventions in Order to Accelerate Economic Development

Evolution of Legislation

Industrial property right (IPR), in its contemporary form, has expanded since the 16th century when Italy, at that time the economic centre of Europe, created the first law meant to protect inventors as well as to attract talented men and their inventions in order to accelerate economic development. In the course of the following centuries, the Italian Model spread through Europe [1] and at the end of the 18th century, most industrial countries had implemented a set of rules on industrial property (IP), more or less inspired by this model.

Today, the new standards of IP are coming from the US. As can be seen from the sectors of biotechnology and information technology, the American legal framework is the basis for the evolution of legislation all over the world and in particular in Europe. The leading American position, in those two fields is largely considered as a justification for the adaptation of the European legal framework, Europe running behind both in biotechnology and information technology.

However, would a clear extension of patentability to new subject matter help Europe to catch up with the US level of development in biotech and information and communication technology (ICT)? On the one hand, this adaptation gives rise to debates, which may be detrimental to the construction of a coherent and unified legal framework while favouring the American lead. On the other hand, whereas today patentability is easy in the US, there is growing doubt about the effective role of patents to stimulate scientific and technical development and innovation. Diverse studies show that the American results in biotech and ICT can be accounted for by a far larger set of factors than the only strengthening of patent laws. What lessons can be derived from this?

In the next section, we will compare industrial property legislation in Europe and the US. We will then analyse the European and US positions in the fields of biotech and ICT. Finally, in the last section, we will present the debates related to the adaptation of industrial property legislation in Europe, for the purpose of strengthening competitiveness in the studied technological fields.

4.3 Protection of Biotech and ICT Inventions: the Diffusion of the American Model

A New Techno-Economic System

Biotech, as well as information technology, has existed in everyday life for a millennium. As a matter of fact, in the general sense of the word, biotechnology refers to techniques and knowledge using living properties for practical and industrial purposes and exist through very old techniques and know-how using yeast or bacteria in order to produce food products (bread, cheese, drinks). In the same way, people have very soon tried to create and improve their means of communication (from the birth of writing, to the telegraph and the telephone...)

However, for thirty years, the scientific and technical improvements in these fields have produced such significant enlargement of their application fields that it is now necessary to propose new definitions meant to facilitate the evaluation and comparison of the levels of development of these scientific and technical fields in different countries. Biotechnology is thus defined (temporarily) by OECD as "the application of science and technology to living organisms as well as their parts, products and models, in order to modify living or non living material in order to produce knowledge, goods and services" [2]. In the same way, in 1998, OECD member countries agreed to define the ICT sector "as the combination of manufacturing and service industries that capture, transmit and display data and information electronically" [3].

Biotech and IT are considered, in the US as well as in Europe, as strategic technologies at the centre of a new techno-economic system because of the multiple and varied applications they promise in very diversified sectors and their role in the renewal of production means (from agriculture to health, to communication, telecommunication and environment). They are also pivotal in the political and legal thinking because of the new questions they ask society (e.g. cloning).

Consequently, issues related to the property of discoveries and creations ensuing from recent scientific and technical progress in these fields are subject to intense legal activity and to debates, which we are going to review in the following parts of this chapter.

From Copyright to Patent: the New Standards of Protection

It was in the 1980's, in a context of decreasing competitiveness and serious challenge by Japanese enterprises, that the US made important changes in the IPR, and notably in these two particular fields. An abundant literature exists concerning this subject and we limit our analysis to the relation of the main steps of this evolution (see No. 99/2002 of *Revue d'économie industrielle*, [4]).

Concerning ICT, the main changes are related to software and business model [5, 6]. In the early 80's, the American legislator tried to protect computer programs through the Copyright Act (Computer Software Copyright Act, 1980) but software publishers considered this evolution as insufficient, because of the difficulty to protect themselves from potential counterfeiting. Then case-law (through the Court of Appeals of the Federal Circuit) lead to the patentability of computer programs (*Diamond v. Diehr*, 1981): until then, as they were composed of mathematical algorithms, computer programs were excluded from patentability, just like natural laws, scientific theories, natural phenomena, abstract ideas, formulae and methods.

Patent granting criteria in the US are as follows: patent is granted to an inventor; it protects an invention and this invention must be useful, new and non-obvious. The notion of non-obviousness is more or less the same as the notion of "inventive activity" used in Europe. On the other hand, the concept of "utility" may sometimes differ from the one of "industrial use". Computer program patentability then ensued from the explanation that a computer program represents an invention (in terms of process), and from the fact that it produces "a useful, concrete and tangible result". This is the same idea that has led courts to accept the patentability of business methods (the main decision in this field is *Street Bank v. Signature*, 1988). Business models are today understood in a wide sense in the US: they include educational, management, e-commerce, counselling, financial methods....

In Europe, the legal framework is much more restrictive, even if there is a strong tendency in favour of accepting to patent computer programs. The Munich Convention (October 5, 1973), in article 52-2, excludes the patentability of computer programs as such, these being protected by copyright, but debates have increased in recent years. The European Patent Office (EPO) has delivered many patents for computer programs considered as technical processes, i.e. as technical inventions. However, software as such (mathematical algorithm) is excluded from patentability. The diplomatic conference held in Munich (November 23-29, 2000) which was to revise the Munich Convention finally decided to keep article 52-2 unchanged.

While an invention including a software program can be patented by EPO or by national offices, the specific modes of enforcement of patentability are different and create obstacles to the exchange of products on the internal market. This is the reason why, in 2002, the European Commission presented a draft-directive on the protection of computer-implemented inventions by patents [7]. Different types of inventions are studied. Those, whose operation involves using a computer program and which make a "technical contribution", in other words which contribute to the state of the art in the technical fields concerned, would be eligible for patents. On the other hand, neither computers as such (in isolation from a machine on which they may run), nor business models that use existing technological ideas and apply them to, for example, e-commerce, would be eligible for a patent. These programs will continue to be protected under copyright law.

Once carried by the European Council and by the Parliament, this directive should be implemented by Member States. Nevertheless, the number of patents granted for computer programs by EPO (more than 30 000 since 1978, when the Convention on European Patent came into force) and the numerous decisions taken on this subject by the Courts of Appeal of the European Patent Organisation, tend to demonstrate that excluding computer programs from patentability is less and less a strict rule.

Appropriation of Living Parts

The origin of the extension of patentability to living organisms can also be found in the US and, in this case, only the decisions of courts of Appeals led to changes [8]. The first important decision is the *Chakrabarty decision* of the Supreme Court of the US: When this employee (A. Chakrabarty) of General Electric filed a patent for a genetically modified micro-organism able to absorb the oil of black tides, the United States Patent and Trademark Office (USPTO) rejected it on the grounds that a micro-organism, as a product of nature, could not be eligible for a patent. After many appeals, the Supreme Court of the US accepted the patent, explaining that this microorganism was not a pure product of nature but that human hands had been used to create it.

121

This decision is then the foundation for patent granting in the US: in other words, every living being produced by a non-natural process (apart from human beings) will henceforth be eligible for patent. It is the case of the patent granted in 1980 to Stanford University for recombinant DNA[1], and subsequently of the patent granted in 1988 to Harvard University for a transgenic animal (the "oncomouse patent"[2]) aimed at being an experience model for cancer research. After these important steps, the 90's were concerned with the patentability of human gene and research tools [9]. The National Institute of Health filed patents related to 2500 DNA sequences, and justified them in mentioning their utility for a purpose of research (these Expressed Sequence Tags EST are used for the identification of genes). It is because this kind of utility is considered as too far from commercial use that USPTO first refused to grant these patents. However, then USPTO revised the utility criteria – Utility Examination Guidelines published since 1995 to 2001 – and has finally accepted to grant patents for DNA sequences considered as useful (tools of research) and for genes involved in disease onset.

In Europe, debates on the legal protection of biotechnological inventions became more intense in the 90's and gave birth to directive 98/44/EC of the European Parliament and the Council of 6 July 1998 which marked out the patentability of genes and of partial sequences of a gene. The first paragraph of article 5 states "the human body, at the various stages of its formation and development, and the simple discovery of one of its elements, including sequence or partial sequence of a gene, cannot constitute patentable inventions". Nevertheless, its second paragraph specifies, "an element isolated from the human body or otherwise produced by means of a technical process, including the sequence or partial sequence of a gene, may constitute a patentable

---

[1] Recombinant DNA is a tool, which permits to handle genes, invented in 1973 by S. Cohen (University of Stanford) and H. Boyer (University of California). "These two researchers have taken two organisms unable to mate naturally, isolated a peace of DNA from each of them and recombined these two pieces of genetic material (...) Recombinant DNA is a kind of biological sewing machine which permits to fasten up each element of the genetic code of organisms which have no link between them", 31, p.44.

[2] This patent concerns a mammal obtained through genetic engineering. Thanks to this handling, this mammal may develop, under certain conditions, some tumours, which are used in the research against cancer.

122

invention, even if the structure of this element is identical to that of a natural element". This directive was the starting point of important debates in Europe: it was to be implemented in the member states before 30 July 2000 and, despite its confirmation by the European Court of Justice in 2001, this directive so far has not been adapted to the law in many member states.

In January 2003, only six member states (Denmark, Finland, the United Kingdom, Ireland, Spain and Greece) had implemented the directive. In December 2002, the Commission decided to request the other nine to do the same on pain of prosecution before the European Court of Justice. The European Patent Office has also incorporated the main provisions of directive 98/44/EC in the implementation regulations to the European Patent Convention (decision of the Administrative Council of 16 June 1999). Consequently, patents for biotechnological inventions are thus granted in compliance with the provisions of the directive[3]. The EPO states in its 2001 annual report that its practises (in terms of patent grants) are subject to criticism[4]. In order to reduce these difficulties, the office has created a special focus group. Today the European framework is still fragmented. However, the recent agreement on community patent (March 2003) and then the creation of a special court in Europe (in 2010) should contribute to reduce these difficulties.

The leading position of the US, in Biotech as well as in the ICT sector is commonly considered as a justification for the evolution of IPRs in Europe. The following point, studying the American and European performance, makes it possible to assess the existing gap in this field between Europe and the US.

---

[3] Moreover, the provisions of the directive used in the implementing regulation also apply to patents granted to Switzerland, Liechtenstein, Monaco, Cyprus, Turkey, the Czech Republic, Slovaquia, Bulgaria and Estonia.

[4] For example, in the case of the patent for the Harvard oncomouse, after 16 years of proceedings, in November 2001 EPO decided to grant the patent but to limit it in comparison with the American patent. According to directive 98/44/EC, animal varieties are not patentable but if an animal can be obtained only through genetic engineering to the exclusion of any natural breeding, the invention relating to such an animal may be protected by patent. In Europe, the oncomouse patent is limited to transgenic rodents with the cancerous gene and not to its extension (as it is the case in the US) to any non-human, transgenic mammal, 13, p.15.

4.4 Comparative Position of Europe and the US in Biotech and Information Technology

Capacity to Invent

In order to measure the performance of a country in a specific technological field, several indicators can be used: patent is an indicator of the capacity to invent; thus, it strongly interests us. However, this capacity to invent (as measured by patents) is, for a part, stemming from a capacity to produce knowledge, whose evaluation is based on the number and the relevance of publications (citations); Once more, scientific production is often stemming from the financial and human means which are devoted to research and also to the creation of new enterprises. Of course, we do not want to reveal some automatic relations, because an important scientific basis does not automatically produce new patents (because the legal rules do not facilitate the creation of patentable inventions; because the knowledge – very basic – is far from practical use; or because other forms of "bridges" are missing, such as engineering services, to transform knowledge into new prototypes). These precautions taken, we will start our observation by comparing the capacities to invent, then we will try to understand to which extent this capacity to invent is correlated (or not) to the respective scientific bases in the studied fields.

Capacity to Invent in Biotech and IT: the Americans Lead the Race and the Europeans are Catching Up

In 2000, the European Commission implemented an *Innovation scoreboard* in which an indicator compares high tech patent applications (the high tech classes include pharmaceuticals, biotechnology, information technology and aerospace) in the Member States of the European Union, to which, notably, the US and Japan were added in the latest version [10]. This indicator is based on patent applications at the USPTO on the one hand and in the EPO on the other hand. It measures the number of patent applications per million population. It shows the American lead for high tech patent applications, at the USPTO as well as in the EPO.

Table 6: High Tech Patent Applications per Million Population (2000 or the Latest Available Date)

	Europe	United States	Japan
USPTO high tech patent applications (per million population)	12.4	91.9	80,0
EPO high tech patent applications (per million population)	27.8	49.5	36.6

Source: [10].

If we observe the specific fields of Biotech and IT, the American lead over Europe appears strongly. Firstly, the growth of patents in the 90's in the fields of biotechnology but also in ICT has been much more important than the growth of patents in all other fields. At the EPO, biotechnology patents increased by 10.5% and by 8% for ICT patents, while total patents rose by 5% during the period 1990-1997.

In these two technological fields, most patents are from the US, more than Europe. 50% of the biotech patents in OECD are coming from the US. However, between 1990 and 1997, European Union has improved its position, increasing year after year the proportion of patents filed in these fields. In 1997, biotech patents accounted for 6% of the total number of patents filed by the US at the EPO, and only 3% for the European Union, which nevertheless gained ground between 1990-1997, as the average annual growth rate of biotech patent applications compared to total patents rose 11.5% in Europe, and 10.8% in the US [11].

Concerning ICT, the European Union and the US are closer since almost 40% of total patent applications filed at the EPO are from European countries, above the shares of the US (34%) and Japan. Nevertheless in 1997, 16,3% of patents filed by US were in IT, against 10% for UE but here again, the European Union seems to be catching up with the US: between 1990 and 1997, the average annual growth rate of patents filed in IT compared with the total number of patents rose 13.4% in the UE and 7.9% in the US [2]. Thus, concerning the invention capacity, the American lead is clear, but the Europeans are obviously catching up if we consider the growth rate of patents filed in the 90's, in biotech as well as in IT.

European and American Scientific Potentials: the "European Paradox"?

The scientific potential of a country can be estimated by its publications and expenditures in the studied fields. These indicators are more disparate than patent indicators. In biotech and IT, the European weakness is often explained not only by an insufficient quantity and quality but also by a great difficulty to commercialise research. In 2000, in all sectors, the European GERD accounted for 1.9% of GDP while the US GERD accounted for 2.7% of GDP. In order to find a solution to this "paradox", the 6th European research program (2002-2006, total budget: 17.5 billion euros) considers the following topics as a priority for research as well as its commercialisation: "Genomics and biotechnology for health" (20.9% of the total research budget reaching 11.3 billion euros), "technology for the information society" (32.1% of the total research budget).

In Biotech and ICT, the European weakness is often considered as tremendous. Modern Biotechnology, as a science, but also as an industry, expanded in the US in the late 70's with the development of genetic engineering, the industrial production of interferon and the birth of enterprises linked to research notably on the West Coast of the US. This model subsequently spread all over the world, and notably to Europe. Comparing the scientific potentials of Europe and the US is not easy. In fact, existing and comparable figures on public R&D expenditures in Biotechnology do not take into account the US and Japan, two countries that invest a lot in this field. In 1997, the OECD member states for which data was available (mainly countries of the European continent, to which Canada and Australia are added) spent about 3.4 billion US dollars (PPP); Germany, the United Kingdom and France accounted for two thirds of these expenditures.

In terms of scientific production, Europe is in a good position: its share in the total number of biotech publications is better than the US share and, for the last ten years, its position has been better and better, whereas the US position has tended to get worse. However, American publications are more cited than European ones [11].

Table 7: Shares of the total number of publications in the biotechnology and microbiology NSIOD journal category 1986-1998 and the relative impact

	Share of the total number of publications - 1986	Share of the total number of publications - 1998	Average relative impact of publications 1986-1988
European countries[5]	37%	40.6%	1.25
United States	22.9%	21%	1.4

Source : [11, 2].

In 2000, the US ICT sector performed 50% of OECD-wide R&D expenditures by the ICT manufacturing sector (figures based only on 19 OECD countries), followed by Japan (21%), Germany (6%), Korea (6%), France (4%) [3]. In the 90's, in countries with data for both manufacturing and service industries, the average growth rates for ICT-related manufacturing R&D expenditures were about 6%, but for ICT-related services, they were about 14%. For ICT industries in 2000, the countries, which had increased their business R&D expenditures, were (in decreasing order of GDP) Finland (more than 1% of GDP), Korea, Sweden, Japan (0.7%), the US (0.6%), Canada, Ireland, the Netherlands, and Germany (around 0.3% of GDP...). For ICT services, the best five spending countries (in percentage of GDP, 2000) were Finland, Sweden, Ireland, Denmark, and the US. Again, the European countries (and notably the largest countries) with a few exceptions are in a bad position.

Capital venture in these fields can also be considered as an interesting indicator because of the particular origin of these industries (notably biotech), which are often linked to research. In the US, which was the first investor in venture capital among the OECD countries with 0.21% of GDP between 1995-1999, high tech sectors (communications, IT, biotech) accounted for 80% of the total spending, against only 30% in Europe (which devoted a little more than 0.05% of GDP to venture

---

[5] Data available for Belgium, Denmark, Finland, France, Germany, Italy, the Netherlands, Spain, Sweden, the United Kingdom, Norway, Switzerland.

capital). We can note that this period was euphoric and that the financial support has now been reduced [2].

Competitiveness: are the US Undisputed Leaders?

The American and European results in terms of competitiveness reflect the American superiority: for example, the US is a net exporter of biotechnology products. In 1999, US biotech exports to OECD countries amounted to more than USD 1.34 billion as compared to USD 970 million for OECD countries. US exports of biotechnology products exceeded imports to a greater degree than was the case for technology products overall. This is suggesting, according to B. Van Beuzekom, [11], that the US have a leading position on the international biotechnology market.

In the ICT sector in 2001 (or latest available date), the share of ICT manufacturing trade (average of imports and exports) is more important for the US (the share of ICT accounts for about 22% in the total manufacturing trade than for Europe (about 18%). We can note that some European countries largely dominate the US in this field; Ireland, Hungary, Finland, the UK- and that Japan and Korea have the most important part (compared to the US and Europe).

On the other hand, the US import more in ICT that they export and only seven countries, among which four from the European Continent, showed a positive ICT trade balance in 2000/2001 (Ireland, Korea, Japan, Finland, Mexico, Hungary, Sweden).The reinforcement of the European competitiveness in these fields requires a global, coherent and unified policy; as a matter of fact, we can observe that European countries have not got the same level of development. In the following part, we will focus on one aspect of this policy, IPRs. In particular, would adaptation of European IPRs to the American model facilitate the European catching up in these fields?

4.5 Is It Worth Copying the American Model?

Stimulate Innovation in the Short Run

Even if the changes made in the legal framework have been quite important in Europe, its legal framework is still fragmented, as we have already mentioned. European results in ICT and biotech are also much contrasted, with leaders (small northern countries notably concerning ICT) and other countries, which are lagging behind (e.g. Portugal or Greece). While the European Parliament and Council have come to the definition of directives, these have not been implemented in many countries.

Two questions arise: what are the consequences of the greater difficulty to patent in the fields of ICT and biotechnology? This raises once again the question of the effects of the adaptation of the European legal framework to the American model: would such an adaptation better stimulate innovation in the short run? What would be the effects in the long run?

The Consequences of the Difficulty to Patent in Europe

We may study two sets of hypotheses dealing with the actual and future effects of the difficulty to patent in Europe in the fields of ICT and Biotech, compared with the greater flexibility of the American regime: the rise in risk and cost of the development of new activities and research in Europe; the European brain drain to the US, explained by the uncertainty (and the relative rigidity) created by the fragmentation of the European legal framework.

The American "Standard-Technology" and Its Consequences; Risk and Cost of Research and Innovation in Europe

The effect of the greater capacity to patent in the US from the 80's has been the increase in the number of patents filed and granted in ICT as well as in biotech; this increase is for a part explained by the "Bayh Dole Act" (1980) which allowed universities to retain patent rights and to offer exclusive licences on inventions developed with federal funds [12].

Such an American lead creates a climate of uncertainty prejudicial to European entrepreneurs. For example, a European software publisher would run the risk of being accused of counterfeiting if he tried to market new software in the US or if he implemented on his website a business model already patented in the US. The cost of lawsuits is moreover (and more so when the lawsuit implies different countries) a prohibitive factor for innovation and creation of new activities.

129

A potential obstacle and an increase of the cost of their activity are added to this uncertainty since American firms have built monopolistic positions on specific parts of knowledge or on research tools. This tendency is particularly marked in the field of biotechnology and especially in genomics. In fact, as M. Cassier explains [9]: "Patents on genes create dependence especially as there is only one genome. It is impossible to get round a monopoly which concerns a gene of disease predisposition (...), unless one discovers another gene which would be more essential to the development of the studied pathology". Every researcher, who would like to use the patented gene, would have to pay royalties to the firm, which holds it... In the same way, the care offer is also dependent on the patent holders, as the strategy of the American firm Myriad Genetics illustrates it. Thanks to its patents on the genes of breast cancer, this firm has built a protected market in the US as well as in Europe for the genetic tests for breast cancer, which were up to that time made freely in hospitals.

However, the Commission pointed out that Directive 98/44/EC is not intended to question the freedom of research in Europe "Under that principle, acts undertaken privately and for non-commercial purposes, as well as acts performed for experimental purposes do not constitute acts of infringement". Moreover another principle exists in all national legislation (as well in the community patent regulation) in the member states of the European community which contains the principle of exempting prior use "which allows anyone who had already used the invention in the European Community, or had made effective and serious preparations for such use, before the patent was filed, to continue such use or to use the invention as envisaged in the preparations" [13].

In ICT, the definition of technical standards and the leading position on the market can also be explained, according to Bekkers, Duysters and Verspagen [14], by a good balance between intellectual property rights and strategic technology agreements. The example they study (GSM) is a leading field for European firms. This kind of study, for example dealing with computer programs would be interesting in order to validate or invalidate our hypothesis. These few examples illustrate the strategy of technological locking, in other words of determining technical and commercial standards by big firms, especially American and Japanese ones (especially concerning ICT as can been seen in the field of MPEG video systems), which may take advantage of

130

the European confusion to establish their technological lead and to monopolise markets. In biotech, The strategy of Myriad Genetics in the field of biotechnology illustrates this increasingly important role of patents in the context of global competition based on innovation.

The Attractive Aspects of the American Market

The absence of a coherent legal framework in terms of industrial property can also be an explicative factor of the attraction of the American market for European firms, researchers and inventors. During the "boom of the new Economy" European entrepreneurs who settled down in the US – especially in order to profit by tax and wage benefits, by venture capital far more abundant than in Europe – got important coverage by the media[6].

According to M. Cervantes and D. Guellec [15], industrial countries are characterised by an important temporary immigration (unlike migration flows between the countries of the South and of the North which last longer) of qualified employees which increased in the last few years. The US are, in absolute terms, the first centre of attraction of foreign skilled workers (40% of US residents born abroad have a high level of education). Since the beginning of the 1990's, about 900 000 skilled workers, in particular computer scientists coming from India, China, Russia an other OECD countries (notably Canada, the United Kingdom and Germany) have migrated to the US with temporary visas and 32% of OECD expatriated students are US residents. A French report from the Senate [16] underlines the growing number of young French high skilled workers expatriated in the US (13% of all expatriated people are in the US, one of the first destinations, after European countries and more than 31% of the expatriated people are in the category of "managerial executives and intellectual professions", i.e. a proportion of managerial executives and intellectual professions more important among the expatriated than among the French working population).

Since the beginning of the 80's, the US has attracted European firms in another way: the number of strategic biotechnology alliances between Europe and the US has largely increased with, according to OECD (CATI database), 5 alliances in 1980 and 47 in 1998. Europe is

---

[6] e.g. in France see *Le Monde*, Les aventuriers de la Silicon Valley, 10 sept 1997, *La tribune*, L'appel de la vallée, 15 octobre 2000.

the first region with which the US has concluded alliances in this field during the covered period [11]. This may be explained firstly by the willingness of European innovative firms not to be excluded from the dynamics and secondly, by the desire of American ones to be aware of the latest European scientific discoveries (we know from another source that within strategic alliances, partners often try to appropriate the produced knowledge, [17, 18]).

In a nutshell, we may assert the hypothesis according to which the lack of clearness and the fragmentation of the European legal framework in terms of IPR play an important role in the standardisation of techniques and the construction of monopolistic positions on markets by the US, which moreover largely attract European capital and human resources. Nevertheless, would the adoption of a legal framework more flexible in terms of patentability improve European competitiveness in the studied fields?

Assets and Limits of the Adoption of a More Flexible Legal Framework of Industrial Property in Europe

The adoption of a more flexible legal framework may perhaps boost the capacity to invent (number of patents filed), since, as we have studied it, the European scientific potential is gaining ground, in terms of scientific production - case of the biotech - and in terms of expenditures in these fields considered as priorities in the European program 2002-2006. Moreover, the Member States of the European Union came to an agreement on March 2003 about the creation of the Community Patent. This agreement may lead to an increase of the number of patents filed. In fact, these patents will be easier to obtain, less expensive (cost divided by two compared to the European Patent) and safer (creation in 2010 of a special Court in Luxembourg which will avoid legal procedures in each country). However, would the only adaptation of IPR be sufficient to stimulate innovation and provoke an increase in the number of patents? On the other hand, what would be the long-term consequences of an intense commercialising of research?

Is Patent the Driving Force of Innovation?

As can be seen for public research (Figure 4), the commercialisation of research depends on different factors organically linked together: regulatory and institutional factors (laws, rules), university strategies, scientific and technical factors, social and economic factors (notably an existing social demand) [19].

Figure 4: The Organic Paradigm of Commercialisation of Research

Legislation
- civil service status of researchers
- mission of universities
- intellectual property rights

University strategy
- development of strategic approaches
- interest of researchers in commercialising research and incentives for them to

Technical progress
- financing of R&D
- leadership in potentially marketable fields

Economic environment and entrepreneurship
- incentives for enterprise creation
- demand for science and technology

Source : [19, 3].

Many enquiries conducted in the US since the beginning of the 80's have stressed, in order to explain the increase of patents filed and granted, the role played by institutional changes: notably the extension of patents to new subject matter, to new institutions, and the role of the "friendly court" (of appeals of the Federal Circuit) [20, 12, 21] or the nature of the university, more open and competitive, which favours the commercialisation of research [22]. However, other reasons are also proposed: scientific and technical reasons (new opportunities opened by IT and biotech; increase of research productivity thanks to the use of information technology, better management of research [23, 24] and, finally, some arguments linked to the strategy of firms (lobbying in order to obtain institutional change, [25]; role of patents in offensive and defensive strategy of firms, ...)

According to these studies, patent is not the only driving force of innovation [26]. Yet its theoretical justification is stemming from its role in stimulating innovation, disclosing scientific and technical information, and facilitating technology transfers. However, once again, the observation of the American regime is at the origin of much critical questioning [27]. Issues refer to the quality of the information disclosed or to the increase of patent litigation which is explained by the high number of patents granted and by the more flexible criteria of patentability (in particular non obviousness and utility[7] and by the large and blurred outlines of patents which include the products of basic research and future developments...). Consequently, if the number of patents granted for twenty years in the US has dramatically increased, it is perhaps not the sign of a good scientific, technical and economic health. For a vast majority of people in Europe, the American model is not a model to follow.

The Commercialisation of Research and Short-Termism: the Consequences in the Long Run

The greater capacity to patent in the field of IT and biotechnology gives birth to more global problems, explained by the characteristics of these fields, which are linked to the products of nature (the gene and its manipulation) and to the products of the spirit (the algorithm and its definition). In particular, in the long run, what are the consequences of this "ultimate" form of private appropriation on the innovation process?

Technical progress is based on the disclosure and the accumulation of knowledge, free and open. "We are dwarfs on the shoulders of the giants," said Isaak Newton and before him, in the Middle Ages, the scholar Bernard de Chartres. This very old precept, the one of "positive externalities" as defined by the contemporary economists (see the theory of endogenous growth) is questioned by the market practice. The patentability of inventions close to or synonymous to scientific discoveries and marketing of research – i.e. the introduction of market oriented rules of functioning and evaluation (first of all productivity and profitability) in scientific research – hinders information disclosure (patent, as we explained above, is no more a guarantee of information disclosure, or more precisely of information of

---

[7] Today, the Utility criteria applies to research results while it was before closely linked to the market; novelty and non-obviousness are also relative. Concerning business models (which is a "new" field of patentability), novelty is not apprehended in relation to the business method as such but in relation to prior patents existing in this field.

high quality), and breaks the virtuous cycle of technical progress in the long run in drying out the common basis of knowledge, which is a guarantee for this cumulative process [28; 29]; see [30] which analyses the different facets of research commercialisation and its consequences.

J. Rifkin [31] explains that American researchers in the field of biotech are very worried about the effects of commercialising research, since the results of their research become trade secrets, patents and because their status of researchers is changed into the one of private consultants and members of administration boards, with for part of them, the advantage of wage increases. As well as for the enterprises, many researchers are attracted by the mermaids' "short-termism". According to a recent report [32] by the *European Commission dealing with the consequences of the directive 98/44/EC* on publications in the field of genetic engineering, researchers (notably coming from University) who declare that patents delay their publications are not used to filing patents. According to this report their lack of experience is the main explanation for the delays. It is right that researchers, especially European ones, are not very aware of industrial property aspects. However, we can argue that this report is only based on the practice of the 6 countries which have implemented the directive (which is little) and that American researchers who have been filing patents for more than 20 years (Bayh Dole Act, 1980) are also worried even if they are used to patents.

Cure people all over the world, feed them and inform them… Is it the objective of commercialising research? In order to answer this question, it is necessary to understand the origins of this new phase of research marketing[8]. It is orchestrated by big firms supported by the rules defined by international institutions. The TRIP agreement (Trade-related Intellectual Property Rights) signed during the Uruguay Round (GATT, 1994) and managed by the WTO (World Trade Organisation) and the WIPO (World Intellectual and Property Rights Organisation) is for a large part the result of firms lobbying (especially in the field of biotech), gathered in an Intellectual and Property Right committee [31].

---

[8] The relations between researchers and enterprises are not new, neither in the US nor in Europe: We could remind, for the anecdote, that the research of Pasteur on fermentation and on "pasteurisation" was supported by brewers, which were very interested in the results of Pasteur's research… It is revealed by the numerous gifts that one of them made to Pasteur, which are exhibited in the Museum of the Pasteur Institute in Paris

This agreement aims at harmonising the intellectual property laws in all member states of the WTO and allows patentability in all technological fields.

For a majority of specialists, it opens the door to a new form of exploitation of genetic resources, which are for a large part situated in countries of the South, as well as to vernacular knowledge of communities in developing countries [31, 33; 34]. This "biopiracy" is added to an "infopiracy" insofar as the greater capacity to patent in the field of ICT will not reduce the numeric break between countries of the North (which are the technology and patent holders) and... the others. The access capacity to information is not only dependent on infrastructure expenditures but also on tools, which permit information storage and treatment, which are more and more patented. This gap between the North and the South also exists within large regions. We may then legitimately ask the question of the consequences of the greater capacity to patent in a Europe already characterised by big differences in its levels of development- especially the technological levels – which will lead to even wider gaps in the near future.

4.6 Conclusion

Adoption of a More Flexible Legal Framework of IPR

As a conclusion, we can say that the American Model in terms of IPR is less and less considered as a model to follow. The US has defined a legal framework favourable to patent holders in the fields of IT and biotech but is now facing new difficulties: large patents granted frantically in fact are not very reliable; infringements are very common and criticism is flooding in about their traditional role of stimulating innovation. On the other hand, the European legal framework is still fragmented, in spite of the harmonisation efforts made by the European Authorities, and Europe is running behind in these strategic fields. However, from 2005 and 2010, the Community Patent should reduce a part of these difficulties, thanks to the reduction of direct costs (patents filing) and indirect ones (creation of a unique Court in Europe).

In fact, IPR cannot be separated from the whole structural competitiveness policy (which includes research, education, competition, defence policies). Europe tries to define global actions, as for example in the field of biotech (see [35] which includes a list of 30 actions: investment in human resources, research, engineering, industrial property, capital venture, creation of networks, information, legal aspects, international co-operation, environment...). *Action No.5 emphasises the implementation of directive 98/44/EC* relative to the legal protection of biotech inventions, which will improve legal security for industry. The clarification of the legal framework in the European community will encourage innovative enterprises using biotechnology to pursue or even to increase their research investments. Nevertheless, the persistence of antagonisms within Europe (for example, the project of a Community Patent was born in the middle 70's and only came to an agreement in march 2003...) often puts a brake on the possibilities of coherent action.

The US can rub their hands: European debates and the fragmentation of its legal framework favour US firms, which carry on patenting and are reinforcing their position on flourishing markets (for example, the total potential of the world market of life sciences and biotechnology applications – apart from farming – is assessed at 2000 billion euros in 2010).

On the other hand, the adoption of a more flexible legal framework of IPR in those two fields leads to an interrogation on the effects of the commercialisation of research in the short term (is patent a stimulation for innovation?) and in the long run (how to conciliate the continuity of technical progress and the reduction of the common fund of knowledge?). It is also necessary to consider the consequences of this flexibility on the differences in terms of development levels, between the countries, which will be able to patent... and the others. This issue applies for the differences in terms of development levels between the countries of the North and those of the South, and those existing within Europe. Larger or not, Europe offers different levels of development. The implementation of a coherent and unified policy of education and research is then a necessity if one wants to avoid the construction of a large Europe, with different speeds of development.

References

1   Volpi R. (2002), *Mille ans de révolutions économiques. La diffusion du modèle italien*, Coll. Economie et innovation, L'Harmattan, Paris.

2   OCDE (2001), Tableau de bord de la science et de l'industrie, Paris.

3   OECDE (2002), Measuring the Information Economy, Paris.

4   *Revue D'économie Industrielle* (2002), Les droits de propriété intellectuelle, nouveaux domaines, nouveaux enjeux, 2ᵉᵐᵉ trimestre, n°99.

5   Lerner J. (2002), Where does State Street Lead? A first look at finance patents, *The Journal of Finance*, vol.LVII, n°2, April.

6   Liotard I. (2002), La brevetabilité des logiciels : les étapes clés de l'évolution jurisprudentielle aux États-Unis, *Revue d'économie industrielle* 99.

7   Commision of the European Communities (2002), Proposal for a directive of the European Parliament and of the Council on the patentability of computer-implemented inventions, (COM 2002) 92 final 2002/0047 (COD).

8   Orsi F. (2002), La constitution d'un nouveau droit de propriété intellectuelle sur le vivant aux États-Unis : origine et signification économique d'un dépassement de frontière, *Revue d'économie industrielle*, 99.

9   Cassier M. (2001), La tendance à la privatisation de la recherche génomique et quelques mesures de régulation et de correction, dans Laperche B. (coord), 2001.

10   Commission Européenne (2002), *Innovation scoreboard 2002*, http://trendchart.cordis.lu

11   Van Beuzekom B. (2001), Biotechnolgy Statistics in OECD Countries: Compendium of Existing National Statistics, STI Working Papers, OECD, 2001/6.

12   Mowery D.C., Nelson R., Sampat B., Ziedonis A. (2001), The Growth of Patenting and Licencing by US Universities: an Assesment of the Effects of the Bayh Dole Act of 1980, *Research Policy* 30,99-119.

13   Commission of the European Communities (2002), Report from the Commission to the European Parliament and the Council. Development and Implications of patent law in the fields of biotechnology and genetic engineering, COM (2002) 545 final.

14   Bekkers R., Duyster G., Verpagen B. (2002), Intellectual Property Rights, strategic technology agreements and market structure. The Case of GSM, *Research Policy*, 31.

15   Cervantes M., Guellec D. (2002), Fuite des cerveaux: mythes anciens, réalités nouvelles, *L'Observateur de l'OCDE*, n°230, janv.

16   François-Poncet J. (2000), *La fuite des cerveaux : mythe ou réalité*, Rapport d'information 388(1999-2000), commission des affaires économiques, Sénat, Paris.

17   Hamel G, Doz Y.L., Prahalad C.K. (1989), Collaborate with your competitors and win, *Harvard Business Review*, vol.67, n°1.

18   Dussauge P., Garette B.(1997), Anticiper les conséquences des alliances stratégiques, *Revue française de gestion*, Juillet-août.

19   Laperche B (2002), The four key factors for commercialising research, *Higher Education Management and Policy*, vol.14, n°3, OECD.

20   Merges R.P.(1992), *Patent Law and Policy*, Charlottesville, Michy Company.

21   Jaffe A.(2000), The US patent System in Transition: Policy Innovation and the innovation Process, *Research Policy*, 29, 4-5.

22   Henrenkson M., Rosenberg N (2001), Designing Efficient Science-Based Entrepreneurship. Lesson from the US and Sweden, *Journal of Technology transfer*, vol.26, 3.

23   Kortum S., Lerner J.(1998), Stronger Protection or Technological Revolution: What is Behind the Recent Surge of Patenting ?, *Carnegie Rochester Conference Series on Public Research*, 48.

24   Etzkowitz H.(1998), The Norms of Entrepreneurial Science: Cognitive Effects and the New University-Industry Linkages, *Research Policy*, 27.

25   Lerner J. (1995), Patenting in the Shadow of Competitors, *Journal of Law and Economics*. 38:2.

26   Laperche B. (2003), *Innovation et brevet : des relations contradictoires*, communication au tables rondes management de l'innovation, Lab.RII, Université du Littoral, 23-24 janvier 2003, forthcoming in D. Uzunidis (ed, 2004), Dynmiques et stratégies d'innovations, De Boeck, Bruxelles.

27   Gallini (2002), The Economics of Patents: Lessons from recent U.S. Patent Reform, *Journal of Economic Perspectives* – VOL.16, n°2, Spring.

28   Foray D. (2000), *L'économie de la connaissance*, Repères, La découverte.

29   Cassier M., Foray D. (2001), Economie de la connaissance: le rôle des consortiums de haute technologie dans la production d'un bien public, *Economie et Prévision*, n°150-151, Octobre-décembre 4/5.

30   *Innovations, Cahiers D'économie De L'innovation* (2003-1) n°17, L'économie du siècle. Points critiques de l'accumulation, Innoval-L'Harmattan.

31   Rifkin J.(1998), *Le siècle biotech*, Pocket, La Découverte.

32   Commission of the European Communities (2002), Report from the Commission to the European Parliament and the Council. An Assesment of the implication for basic genetic engineering research of failure to publish or late publication of, papers on subject s which could be patentable as required under Article 16(b) of directive 98/44/EC on the legal protection of biotech invention COM (2002) 2 final

33   Zerda-Sarmiento A., Forero-Pineda C. (2002), Les droits de propriété intellectuelle sur le savoir des communautés ethniques, *Revue Internationale des sciences sociales*, n°171.

34   Forero-Pineda C., Jaramillo-Salzar H. (2002), L'accès des chercheurs des pays en développement à la science et à la technologie internationales. *Revue internationale des sciences sociales*, Unesco/érès, n°171.

35   Commission Des Communautés Européennes (2002), *Life sciences and Biotech. A Strategy for Europe*, COM 27 final.

36   Laperche B. (coord. 2001), *Propriété industrielle et innovation*, Economie et Innovation, L'Harmattan, Paris.

5

Next Generation Networks and Services: Regulation vs. Self-Regulation/Co-Regulation

5.1 Introduction

This chapter look at how the world economy is moving in transition, i.e. from the industrial age to a new set of rules, that of the so-called "Information Society", which is rapidly taking shape in different aspects of the every-day life. One of the most perceptible impacts of the rapid development of the multiple information and communications digital technologies (in particular those of the high-speed infrastructure supporting the fundamental convergence's aspects) has been on the legislative process. The future regulatory framework has significant importance for any further development.

European governments, Administrations and Local/Regional Authorities, have very early recognised that the "new economy" and particularly the Internet, poses major and critical challenges to the existing regulatory frameworks. The "new" economy is in fact, the complex "product" of rapid progress in digital technologies and accelerated economic globalisation, while it has multiple dimensions, such as technological, regulatory, economic, political, cultural, etc; at the same time, as for the European Union's Member States, the social character of the applied policies towards forming a Single and Unified Market, also becomes a distinct and significant driving force.

At the heart of the regulatory process are also the National Regulatory Authorities (NRAs), which provide the necessary interface for implementing Community principles in line with national legal frameworks and market conditions, preserving a degree of flexibility in a rapidly changed environment.

5.2 Next Generation Infrastructure/Services

Rules of the Game

The Internet is, with no doubt, a cross-border medium where new ways of doing business are developing continuously. It is very quickly changing the market context and the *de facto* "rules of the game", posing significant problems for issues like, for example, the intellectual property rights (IPRs) relevant to the content transmitted and/or received, the protection of data and privacy, e-commerce transactions, electronic contracts, e-payment, information security, encryption, taxation, liability issues and consumer protection which require immediate solutions. As a consequence, the current process of drawing up conformant legislation needs to be accelerated.

Next generation infrastructure/services bring into play a series of important issues in the field of jurisdiction and applicable law at global level. Although progress takes place, it could be occasionally harmed by probable restrictions and/or limitations of specific nature, observed at different levels of the playing ground. The new market structure practically imposes new roles for any of the participants (either residential or corporate), promotes competitiveness and demonstrates the necessity for the re-examination of all terms for the on-line access, use and possession of information. However, market feedback implies that more action is needed in certain regulatory areas; although not a simple task, this has to be made under common well-defined & objective criteria and full transparency. Nowadays, the rapid development of dispute settlement systems and codes of conduct in the European Union (and at global level as well) becomes a matter of urgency to increase business predictability and consumer confidence in many areas, such as the e-Commerce and other innovative sectors of the Information Society Technologies (IST) sector.

Until very recently, regulation and self-regulation perspectives were often seen as diametrically opposed. Pressures from the "new economy" have changed that option - leading to a high degree of consensus on this pragmatic approach. In a fast moving environment, self-regulation has been advocated by industry as a strong tool, which is better adapted to answer the dual challenge of rapidly increasing speed and scope; i.e. a tool to better deliver solutions in the fast-changing global economy. The European Commission backs self-regulation as a flexible, efficient and cost-effective alternative to regulation in many areas, achieving the same results without the delays of a time-consuming "pure" lawmaking process. Of course, certain clear conditions must be met: Self-regulation is a complementary element to the current legislation; it must be in conformity with, and backed by law; it must be enforceable and verifiable. A major development in this respect is the concept of "cooperative approach to governance" or "co-regulation"; the latter takes self-regulation one-step further, i.e. to follow the requirements of the global development. Beyond the mere coexistence of regulation and self-regulation, it implies the sharing of responsibilities between public and private partners, through negotiated agreements, to address a number of challenges. However, for any case, transparency, openness and consensus criteria are important to enjoy the necessary confidence. Co-regulation empowers self-regulation by placing it in a wider clear framework, to mutually reinforce each other. The work also discusses some relevant aspects, mainly arising from the recently proposed new European telecommunications regulatory package, with particular emphasis given to the promotion of measures for competitiveness, cohesion and innovation in various domains of the electronic communications market. Among these initiatives we discuss certain aspects such as those relevant to the E-commerce, the protection of privacy and of personal data as well as aspects for security, for content dispersion and for Intellectual Property Rights (IPRs). For any regulatory activity (including self-regulation and/or co-regulation), the mutual cooperation of the involved parties is more than necessary, while different forms of partnerships can further contribute to the promotion of the common EU policies.

5.3   The Transitional State of the Global Economy

Rapid Emergence of Electronic Commerce

The world economy is moving in *transition*, i.e. from the industrial age to a new set of rules - that of the so-called "Information Society", which is rapidly taking shape in different multiple aspects of the every-day life: the exponential growth of the Internet, the explosion of mobile communications, the rapid emergence of electronic commerce, the restructuring of businesses in all sectors of the modern economy, the contribution of digital industries to growth and employment etc., are some amongst the current features of the new global reality.

Modern social structures are being characterised by continuous changes and evolutionary processes, which are taken place at various levels and sectors. Although there may be occasionally some specific obstacles, the global development is being performed by very fast rates, able to overpass any probable theoretical prediction. Changes are usually underpinned and accelerated by technological progress and globalisation. As the latter can be considered in a more extended framework (including various aspects such as of technological, cultural political and economic nature) it provides many opportunities for the widespreading of the corresponding developing actions, with particular emphasis given to the efficient forwarding of knowledge via different forms of information. More specifically, the combination of global competition and digital technologies is having a sweeping effect on the economy. Digital technologies facilitate transmission and storing of information, while they provide fundamental access facilities without significant costs. As digital information may be easily transformed into economic and social value, it offers huge opportunities for the development of new products and services.

Within the wider sector of the relevant activities, a major role is being performed by different innovations taken place through the global and extended development of the Internet[1]. Simultaneously, the Internet penetrates to all sectors of our life and practically constructs a "global platform" with multiple capacities, able to support provision of innovative services and transfer of digital content. An overview of the current activities of the technological market(s) proves that the various categories of market players involved to the relevant sector(s), react dynamically to the modern challenges; i.e. they both attempt to improve and to develop further, most of their services already offered to the consumers/users, as well as to extend their potential activities to the level of the design and the exploitation of new opportunities. This option constitutes a primary target, as the Internet finally becomes a complex "entity" consisting of modules of distinct and specific building blocks, such as various elements of existing network infrastructure (e.g. cable, wireless, terrestrial, satellite, etc.), different types of services and applications (including multimedia applications and facilities), various forms of digital "content" (which can be expressed as data, text, still images, video, audio-visual, as well as different data bases where users can have access to), software, and other related domains.

Information becomes the key-resource of the digital economy. Companies in different sectors have started to adapt to the new economic paradigm - restructuring to become e-businesses. The corresponding activities cover an extended range of existing market players, varying from digital industries to small and medium enterprises (SMEs). The key to these *e-companies* is their ability to embrace the Internet, to use it to increase their productivity and to widen their market reach, as well as to broaden their worldwide presence. Without any doubt, the Internet has become the moving *"engine"* of the new economy.

---

[1] Up-to-now different and various definitions have been proposed for the "Internet". A most convenient one could be summarised as follows: "Internet can be understood as the global collection of computer & electronic networks with a common system of address based on the Internet Protocol (IP), physically linked by telecommunications infrastructure, supporting packet-based communication between disparate electronic platforms and operating systems, controlled by the TCP/IP suite of protocols". [Defined in Australian Competition and Consumer Commission, Telecommunications Group: "Discussion paper Internet interconnection: Factors affecting commercial arrangements between network operators in Australia", 17 February 2000, p.3].

5.4 The Broader Perspective of Convergence

Multi-Dimensional Reality of "Digital" Convergence

Convergence[2] is amongst the core principles of Information Society developments. It is a phenomenon with multiple dimensions, technological but also economic, regulatory, social, political, cultural, etc. Technological developments associated with digitalisation of information make it possible to dissociate specific communication networks from specific types of information: voice, data, images, etc. All of them can be increasingly transported through all networks and accessed from a variety of terminal equipment. This stimulates market competition and innovation.

From the global experience gained up to the present day, it is commonly evident that we are all living a multi-dimensional reality of "digital" convergence[3] between the different forms of modern technologies (particularly between infrastructure and the various versions of services/facilities offered through them). Digital technologies are the "path" for the provision of either traditional or innovative communications services, offered by different sectors such as telecommunications, broadcasting, media information and information technology (IT). These domains are currently exploiting further possibilities for their interoperability and their mutual inter-working, specifically for many Internet-based applications. This task has a much more important aspect, under the significant evolution of the broadband challenge, able to offer high-speed services of enriched and high quality, for the purpose of the digital inclusion.

---

[2] See the Green Paper on the *Convergence of the Telecommunications, Media and Information Technology Sectors, and the Implications for Regulation towards an Information Society Approach* (COM(97)623).

[3] The term "convergence" eludes precise definition, but it is most commonly expressed as: (i) the ability of different network platforms to carry essentially similar kinds of services; and (ii) the coming together of consumer services such as the telephone, television, and personal computer. This latter expression is most often cited in the popular press, it is easily understood by consumers and has the added interest of reflecting a wider struggle between computer, telecommunications and broadcasting industries for the control of future markets. Despite this popular image however, any convergence of consumer devices is still today much less real than network convergence.

These technology and market developments also have a great potential for *"social convergence"* and collective welfare, in that they remove barriers to communication and facilitate widespread access to information. In short, the convergence phenomenon has implications that go well beyond information technology: it is transforming society, that is, the way companies operate, and individuals behave and interact with each other and so on.

However, there is the danger that many people and regions remain excluded from the Information Society that is emerging, so that social and regional gaps widen rather than the opposite. This originates from the fact that for the completion of all necessary activities, significant investments have to be made by both public and private sector, to cover most of the regions, not only those of significant business interest. Public authorities should take the distance necessary to make objective analysis. They have to establish clear political priorities and policies in pursuit of long term general interest goals, which should remain relatively unaffected by short-term market fluctuations. This should be done in a way that is compatible with the objective of attracting the necessary investments from the private sector. Within such a framework of reference, it becomes more than obvious that the existence of clear and well-defined regulatory principles and corresponding measures could be a significant guarantee and a basic factor to ensure, *under suitable terms*, further development.

5.5 Technological Development and Globalisation of Information Society

Information Leads to the Creation of Knowledge

Modern development is also realised through the combined contribution of distinct sectors and applications originating from the Information Society; this practically formulates a complex environment of social and economic evolution, where the acquisition, the storage, the evaluation, the transfer and the spreading of information leads to the creation of knowledge and to the fulfilling of the needs of the citizens (or other parties), while at the same time it contributes to the development of commercial and business activities, the production of goods and the improvement of the living standards.

In order to ensure equal, objective and non-discriminatory terms and opportunities for the global development, up to the present day, most of such activities have been performed (and still are) under the supervision of the State, to avoid possible distinctions and to provide "reasonable" terms for the use of the new technologies. In particular, the European Union has gradually promoted a series of adequate measures, either specific policies or regulatory provisions of general and/or of detailed nature, to guarantee the healthy market development for the different Member States. It is obvious that such initiatives or actions have a strong and extended impact, as their results do not only concern technological options but also affect the total market, any forms of business activities and interactivity with society as well.

The penetration of modern infrastructure and services, using the Internet as the basic means, constitutes a strong source of potential for the improvement of the standards of the citizens, while under suitable terms and conditions it may contribute to the evolution of regions, providing more competitive performance options to the markets (local, national or global). As for the European reality, the appearance of new services and the modernisation of the existing ones by several market players, is expected to extend the entire information market dimensions and to offer more selections and benefits either for service providers or for end users (private and/or corporate).

The global character of the existing communication platforms, and especially the Internet, constitute the basic key for further completion of the world economy; this offers many opportunities and challenges, as the relatively low costs for presence to the world wide web (www) provide the option either to enterprises (independently of their size) to have regional or international presence or to the consumers to obtain more benefits from the wider range of products and services offered. One of the most important reasons of the successful penetration of the Internet is that it provides adequate access to innovative applications. Moore's Law[4] states that the processing power of

---

[4] As has been initially stated in 1965, by Gordon Moore, one of the founding members of the international "network" called then as the "Intel". The statement was about the increasing speed of the transistors' density in unified circuitries. Today, such computer density doubles every 1,5 year and has direct results upon the prices and the performance of the computer unified circuits. Many experts estimate that the above situation will remain valid at least for one more decade.

microprocessors doubles every 18 months. However, the development of the information and communications technologies (ICT) is much faster; i.e. a characteristic example is the fact that the volume of data transferred via the Internet is doubled, almost every year.

5.6 The Necessity for the Improvement of the Regulatory Framework and Adaptation to Current Challenges

Single Market Legislation

The future regulatory framework has significant importance for any further development. Improving the existing regulation has been on the European Commission (the "Commission") agenda since the 1980s. 1992 Single Market legislation was a prime example of an action to improve the regulatory environment for European businesses and citizens.

The New Approach[5] was launched in the 1980s and has been widely applied ever since. This is a concept of flexible legislation based on a high level of protection, which supports innovation and competitiveness. Essential requirements, which must be met, are specified in the relevant directives but industry has wide flexibility in how it meets these targets. Other initiatives on better regulation are for example the Business Impact Assessment (BIA) for new legislation and

---

[5] The Council Resolution of 7 May 1985 introduced *"A New Approach to Technical Harmonisation and Standards"*. Its aims were to establish a level playing field for the freedom of movement of products on the internal market, while guaranteeing a high level of protection. The New Approach also proposed to leave the definition of the detailed rules, which would be one way of assuring the compliance with the essential requirements, to the economic actors of the framework of the European standardisation structures, i.e. *"not to regulate for the sake of regulation, but to harmonize only when and where necessary"*.

149

the SLIM initiative[6] to simplify and improve existing Internal market regulations.

Since their inception, the objective of the EU's telecommunications policies has been to encourage the provision of high quality services at low prices to European citizens. The Commission has used liberalisation and harmonisation rules[7] to create the conditions for a competitive and dynamic internal market in which new entrants would be able to develop services and push prices down. To this end, all segments of the telecoms market have been gradually liberalised. The full liberalisation of services and infrastructures in Member States came in January 1998; since then there was a substantial market growth and increasing competition. Furthermore, interested parties have been participated to various "open" consultations through different instruments, such as Green Papers, White Papers, public hearings, and, increasingly, the Internet. An important case is the new Telecommunications Package[8], which was developed on the basis of widespread consultations and adopted in December 2001 - within the ambitious time limit set out by the EU Lisbon Summit[9]. The result was an entirely regenerated framework for the wider telecommunications sector, able to face the new challenges, especially due to the rapid development of electronic communications services. At the same time,

---

[6] The SLIM initiative (simpler legislation for the internal market) is one of the pilot projects to simplify national and Community legislation relating to the internal market.

[7] Characteristic is the case referred to the telecommunications sector, where two main categories of European Directives have gradually become into force: The "Liberalisation" Directives based on the initial Directive 90/388/EEC *on competition in the market for telecommunications services* (OJ L192, 24.07.1990, p.10), and the "Harmonization" Directives based on the initial Directive 90/387/EEC on the establishment of the internal market for telecommunications services through the implementation of open network provision (ONP) (OJ L192, 24.07.1990, p.1).

[8] See, for example, http://europa.eu.int/comm/information_society/policy/framework/index_en.htm.

[9] See, for example, Commission Report *"eEurope - An Information Society For All"* (6978/00), as well as Presidency Conclusions of the Lisbon European Council. Also consider Commission Communication "*Realising the European Union's Potential: Consolidating and Extending the Lisbon Strategy*", COM(2001) 79 final.

some relevant measures have been promoted for the sector of the broadcasting emissions.

The Commission has been actively monitoring these developments. As a result of the liberalisation initiatives, telecommunications services became the fastest growing sector of the European economy[10]. Competition keeps intensifying, leading to lower prices, more choice, better quality of service and innovation. Allied to the development of new technologies and markets, this means that there has been a fundamental shift in the environment in which the EU policies operate. There has also been a radical change in thinking on the part of governments concerning the role of communications technologies in social and economic development. The EU has been embarked on a drive to become a dynamic and competitive knowledge-based economy.

The Challenging for the NRAs

As regards transposition of the framework, national legislation has been consolidated in bringing increased clarity and legal certainty. At the heart of the regulatory process are the National Regulatory Authorities (NRAs), which provide the necessary interface for implementing Community principles in line with national legal frameworks and market conditions. They have increasing expertise and authority in regulating the sector. The results are evident in the market, where the choice of services and suppliers continues to expand and prices to decrease. In some European Member States work is already under way to adapt the regulatory authorities to the converged electronic communications environment, in some cases by increasing coordination with the national competition authorities or assigning competition powers to the NRAs. Increased cooperation between NRAs at European level is an encouraging precursor to coordination under the new framework.

Among the most crucial issues facing regulators, apart from the need to refine and clarify their own methods of operation, are currently competition in local access in particular for broadband, call termination charges in mobile networks, flat rate interconnection for internet access, the pricing and provisioning of leased lines, general tariff and cost

---

[10] See, for example, *7th Report on the Implementation of the Telecommunications Regulatory Package*, COM(2001) 706, 26.11.2001.

accounting principles, and the roll-out of third generation mobile networks. Questions also continue to revolve around numbering, universal service, rights of way and the transposition of the data protection directive. A significant factor for further success is to guarantee adequate assignment of powers to NRAs and the ability to resolve disputes rapidly.

5.7 Existing or Potential Limitations Preventing from Development

Immediate Regulatory Response

It could be expected, however, that the continuous development of new services (including the Internet), which combines elements from the previous mentioned sectors (but which is not necessary limited to them), could be occasionally harmed or prevented from any probable restrictions and/or limitations, observed at different levels of the entire market.

Where there exist probable restrictions of regulatory nature, it is not necessary to consider that there should be some kind of immediate regulatory response, under the supervision of the NRA(s), without investigating any other potential solutions. In particular, the appliance of the healthy competition rules is of significant importance, and any of the proposed policies should be based upon such standards. However, in some cases, alternative solutions could be promoted from the market itself; the different market players become able to understand the specific issues affecting their global set of activities and, they may become able to propose, from their experiences, transitional measures for at least short-termed or medium-termed solutions. Such initiatives should be realised in a cooperative environment, under transparent, objective and well-defined evaluation criteria and under the supervision of the official regulatory authorities.

As for the EU Member States, for any particular issue, there should be an adequate and exact estimation of any existing and/or potential limitations preventing from the full applicability of the EU Treaty, with major emphasis given to the development and the effective creation of an internal single market (also including the wider European Economic Area - EEA), the promotion of competitiveness, the lowering of prices, the improvement of quality and the protection of the consumers' interests.

There are different options as for the sufficiency of any of the existing regulatory frameworks (at European and national level), able to describe a continuously transformed environment, with results observed for a variety of sectors. According to a first approach, the development of new products and services is being prevented from probable regulatory uncertainty: i.e. the fact that any existing specific rules have been set out for an environment of national scale, for technologies which are not always considered as entirely innovative and for conditions of "limited" competition (which do not reflect a fully liberalised market), while at the same time, services and applications drastically penetrate various of the existing market sectors, via different forms of infrastructure and without restrictions imposed by the sense of the national frontiers. Such an approach concludes that any specific regulatory uncertainty acts as a negative factor for the realisation of different investments and, *as a consequence*, affects the perspectives for the implementation of the Information Society.

According to a different second approach, the particular features of different technical sectors are fundamental factors able to define, more accurately and more restrictively, the range of the convergence between services offered to the public. This option becomes more important due to the fact that a service can be finally offered to the end-user, independently of the technical means used. This implicates that any regulatory initiative should be primarily focused upon the financial terms and conditions for the provision of a service, in order to ensure efficiency, performance and quality targets.

5.8 New Market Conditions – Corporate and Residential Points of View

Wide Range of Commercial Transactions

The continuous convergence processes, the opening of the European telecommunications sector to the competition, the fast development of Internet and the global penetration of on-line electronic services, have created a completely new market structure, implicating new roles for any of the participants. As for the operators, the relevant business

153

activities represent a wide range of commercial transactions, varying from probable "horizontal" alliances/collaborations (or even occasionally mergers) between different enterprises or organisations for the minimisation of the investment risks to a behaviour of a "vertical" activation, as some players already exercising their activities to specific market sectors attempt to gain more benefits from convergence and to extend their presence to other domains (or to develop economies of scale). Under such a framework, it should be expected that the common European competition rules will continue to play a primary role, for the evaluation of any existing business activity or any initiative.

The Commission has promoted various policies either for encouraging technical innovation or for the promotion of commercial (and of other) agreements, as for the entrance and for further activation of new players in the markets. To ensure objective terms, the Commission has taken measures able to prevent from any particular agreements or activities leading to anti-competitive behaviour, while extended control has been exercised for those having dominant or even significant market position, to avoid any potential abuse effects.

As for the citizen consumer/user, the new technologies, and especially the Internet, have started to change the way of living and the methods of communication. Internet has been transformed to a basic "tool" for global communication as well as to an extended "platform" for transactions. It also offers positive benefits for many activities, by empowering consumers, lowering the barriers to the creation and distribution of content and offering wide access to even richer sources of digital information[11].

In a medium-term basis, it is estimated that most of the population will have access to Internet and will use most of the relevant facilities. Residential users do not use the Internet only as a means for their entertainment, but also for communication, for educational purposes and access to information, for contacting public authorities and for other business purposes as well. The case of the recent development of the e-commerce[12] probably illustrates one of the most important and

---

[11] See, for example, Decision No 276/1999/EC of the European Parliament and of the Council of 25 January 1999, adopting a multi-annual Community action plan on promoting safer use of the Internet by combating illegal and harmful content on global networks (OJ L33, 06.02.1999, p.1).

[12] See Directive 2000/31/EC of the European Parliament and of the Council of 8 June 2000 ("E-Commerce Directive"), OJ L178, 17.07.2000, p.1.

characteristic examples, while it demonstrates effective projection to future dimensions.

The relevant market experiences a continuous evolution, without being able to outline, the extension of the detailed influences it exercises. Technology faces many challenges to respond, as fast as possible, to a variety of requirements such as for quality, speed and security perspectives; however technology is not the unique dimension, as there are also other important aspects to take into account. It should be necessary to achieve a degree of synchronisation between the different options, to reach to the best expected result. This is also applied to the case of any attempt for regulation, where many factors originating from different sectors have to contribute.

There is a strong estimation that in the forthcoming future, there will be a domination of market schemes mainly oriented to the provision of value-added services through the Internet. The rapid and global development of Internet implicates significant transformations and major opportunities. However, there are many regulatory issues related to the on-line provision of services, still pending. The present clause simply intends to outline some specific and characteristic cases, among the existing vast majority. Particular emphasis has been given to sectors related to the E-commerce, while for the rest there is an indicative reference. The aim is to provide some fundamental examples for sectors where regulatory initiatives will be of major significance.

The European Commission has defined electronic commerce as any business that is carried out electronically[13]. This includes electronic trading in goods and services, on-line delivery of digital content, electronic fund transfers, electronic share trading, electronic bills of lading, commercial auctions, on-line sourcing, public procurement, and direct consumer marketing and after sales service. Electronic commerce can be either "direct" (e.g. on-line ordering, payment and delivery of intangible goods and services such as computer software or information) or "indirect" (electronic ordering of tangible goods which must be physically delivered through traditional channels).

Another significant domain of activities refers to electronic contracts. Contracts negotiated, concluded and executed electronically, *in particular standard form contracts*, raise issues relating to the identity of the parties, the time and place in which the contract was

---

[13] Commission Communication: "A European initiative in electronic commerce" COM(97)157 of 16 April 1997.

concluded and the terms and conditions of the contract. Other issues such as the applicable law, jurisdiction, recognition and enforcement of contracts, currently covered by mechanisms set in international conventions[14] will have to be adapted as well. Contracts are part of private law, hence are not as such within the mandate of the EU. Nevertheless, with respect to contracts affecting issues such as competition, certain financial services and consumers, regulation is in place. These measures, some of which need to be adapted to electronic commerce, address issues relating to contracts negotiated at a distance[15], unfair terms in consumer contracts[16], *and in the future,* financial services contracts.

Electronic payment constitutes another significant domain of activities. This is a complex task incorporating some of the major issues such as: (i) transparency requirements; (ii) issuance of electronic money[17]; (iii) security of payments; (iv) competition and fraud issues. Furthermore, commercial communications (e.g. the advertisements) are an important element in the development of E-commerce as certain services (e.g. content on the Internet) are dependant of them. Some basic security issues may implicate cryptography issues for the protection of services on a conditional access basis[18], encryption and digital signatures issues[19], while IPRs can refer either to copyright[20] (e.g. reproduction right, communication to the public, distribution right, rights management information), to databases[21], to trademarks and

---

[14] For example, the Rome convention on the law applicable to contractual obligations, the Hague and Vienna conventions on sale of goods and the Brussels and Lugano conventions on jurisdiction and the enforcement of judgements in civil and commercial matters.

[15] Directive 97/7/EC of 20 May 1997 *on the protection of consumers in respect of distance contracts,* OJ L144, 1997, p.19.

[16] Directive 93/13/EEC of 5 April 1993, *on unfair terms in consumer contracts.*

[17] See, Directive 2000/46/EC of 18 September 2000, *on the taking up, pursuit of and prudential supervision of the business of electronic money institutions* (OJ L275, 27.10.2000, pp.39-43).

[18] Directive 98/84/EC, *on the legal protection of conditional access services* (OJ L320, 28.11.1998, p.54).

[19] Directive 99/93/EC of 13 December 1999, *on a community framework for electronic signatures* (OJ L13, 19.01.2000, pp.12-20).

[20] See, for example, Directive 2001/29/EC, on the harmonisation of copyright and related rights in the information society (OJ L167, 22.06.2001, p.10).

[21] Directive 96/9/EC *on the legal protection of databases* (OJ L77, 1998, p.20).

domain names or to Internet hypertext links. Other matters, of particular commercial importance, may be referred to liability issues or to taxation issues.

5.9   The Results Upon the European Regulatory Framework

Weaknesses of the Existing Regulation - Need for New Measures

The new reality imposes the necessity for the re-examination of all terms for the on-line access, use and possession of data and information. The need for new rules, such as for the protection of privacy and of personal data[22], for the commercial use of material suitably protected by intellectual property rights (IPRs), etc., is more than simply obvious. For such a hard task there are usually confronted options as, *in fact*, the protection of information may oppose to the commercial exploitation of information. Any acceptable and applied solution should be based upon a sort of equivalence between any relevant benefits.

The transformation of the society, of the State and of the economy, due to the rapid technological development, radically imposes crucial challenges not only for the adequacy of the existing regulatory framework but also for the classical models of legal thinking and legal treatment. Furthermore, it requires the reorientation from the traditional regulatory issues originating from the industrial era to those generated by the Information Society.

Without underestimating the importance and the difficulties implicated by the creation/formulation of new regulations for a multidimensional market still evolving, Member States should redefine, *totally or partially*, their roles in both the real and the virtual world, and they should adopt policies able to lead them closer to the exact needs of the digital era. More specifically, during the latest decade there has been observed a strong and active interest, in particular by many governmental organisations, in order to investigate the effects resulted from the development and the penetration of the Internet market. It

---

[22] Directive 2002/58/EC, "*on the protection of privacy in electronic communications sector*" (OJ L201, 31.07.2002, pp.37-47), as replaced Directive 97/66/EC (OJ L24, 30.01.1998, p.1).

seems[23] that for some critical issues, such as for competitiveness, security and IPRs, much more questions have been created than answers. Furthermore, it looks that for some other matters, such as for the illegal and harmful content[24] on the Internet, the protection of minors and of human dignity (in relation to audiovisual and information services made available to the public), most of the EU Member States have already developed series of measures for the protection of the citizens.

As a result, becomes the need for a regulatory vision aiming to serve the entire society as a single entity, capable to respond either to the needs of the market via the creation of a proper environment for e-business requirements or to the needs of individual users who demand, by the State, services of higher quality[25]. The latter perspective may be extended to various governmental activities, such as social and economic development via e-transactions, e-government applications, health care on-line applications, respect and assurance of legal rights of any party involved to the "digital" reality, etc. Within the context of the current digital reality, *as outlined above*, both the legal provisions of the existing law and the new regulatory initiatives (including draft proposals for regulation) are challenged to establish a "thin" equivalence between two very significant targets:

1. The protection of a series of fundamental rights including, *inter-alia*, access to information, privacy, intellectual and industrial property, safety, assurance of suitable working conditions and consumer's rights.

2. The creation of a legal and regulatory framework, able to encourage the production of new services/facilities and the

---

[23] Currie W. L. (1999) Meeting the Challenge of Internet Commerce: Key Issues and Concerns. Proceedings of the *5th International Conference of the Decision Sciences Institute: Integrating Technology and Human Decisions: Global Bridges into the 21st Century*. D. K. Despotis and C. Zopounidis (Eds.). July 4-7, 1999, Athens, Greece.

[24] Council Recommendation of 24 September 1998 on the development of the competitiveness of the European audiovisual and information Services industry by promoting national frameworks aimed at achieving a comparable and effective level of protection of minors and human dignity (98/560/EC), (OJ L270, 07.10.1998, p.48).

[25] See, for example, *e*Europe 2005: An Information Society for All, An Action Plan, COM(2002) 263 final, 28.05.2002.

economic development as well, under the full operational scope of the Information Society applications.

A first limitation (or difficulty) may be focused on the exact determination of the nature of services produced, transferred and commercially offered within the wider framework of the Information Society. The rules, the entire configuration of the regulation and the methods for producing legislation are still influenced by some features of the traditional industrial society. Many basic principles and existing mechanisms (such those for the licensing regimes), which have been successfully used for the traditional (but distinct) domains of telecommunications and broadcasting, are not always convenient to face the modern requirements imposed by convergence and competitiveness.

A second difficulty for regulatory intervention refers to any potential uncertainties of the regulator's entity, due to the fact that the corresponding object is not a static one; on the contrary it is variable, not completely known in full detail and it is always subsequent to a continuous evolutionary process. It is not possible to regulate, in advance, an object, which gradually alters and/or changes. However, mutual interactivity and experience gained from other sectors may provide a higher probability for the final success. This is the reason why in the global "sphere" of the Internet (and of the Information Society), every detailed regulatory provision is, *by definition*, of "temporary" nature. The rate for the production of regulation is slower than the rate of the evolution of technologies (and of markets), and in some cases the existing legal provisions have to be reconsidered to adapt to the current states of technology. As a result, there is a continuous demand for the effective "renewal" of the regulatory provisions and of the regulatory tools themselves, as well.

As a consequence, the current regulatory framework presents two major defects, reducing its ability and making difficult its effectiveness: on the one hand it is oriented to the regulation of "static" states, which are evolving and changing by relatively slow rates, and on the other hand it refers to situations of the existing world, while most of the activities are realised in a virtual reality. As a result, the regulatory responses are necessarily of temporal nature, while at the same time, network technology provides options for a global character to communications and to the markets. There is a strong reservation, as for the adequate efficiency of the national regulatory schemes, to arrange most of the challenges raised. Compared to the common and well-defined European regulatory provisions, any probable inconsistencies or deviations of the national legislations may be harmful for achieving positive results.

The universal character of the Internet points out the potential difficulties for the appliance of the regulatory provisions from a Member State to a third country. The fast rate of changes constitutes a hard challenge for any potential regulatory initiative, as services and products change in weeks (or in months), while regulatory solutions at community level are taken place in a scale measured in months (or in years) correspondingly. However, the global presence of the Internet provides the ability to impose, at a certain degree, some particular policies for regulatory actions at national level.

The need for the treatment of the previous mentioned problems imposes the adoption of investigation activities for "technologically neutral" regulatory solutions[26] together with the usage of novel techniques as basic tools for the successful forwarding of general law's applications. In many particular cases, technology may directly correspond to any request for protection (e.g. privacy, rights, intellectual property) while it may produce new methods for the control of content distribution. In any case, the combination of regulatory and other alternative -and friendly- technological solutions may guarantee the protection of the citizens.

As a concluding remark, global solutions are significantly important, although they may result from long, complex and extremely extended processes. However, global agreements are welcomed as they correspond to commonly accepted guidelines. On the other hand international cooperation is necessary, *even if the relevant progress is slow*, particularly for the promotion of activities such as intellectual property or the e-commerce. During the transitional phases, there will be probably some "parallel" (but not necessarily conflicting) systems of law. For the particular sectors where the traditionally existing regulatory framework(s) will not be able to solve appearing challenges, it should be necessary to develop innovative options suitable either for regulations' modernisation referred to recent services or for the creation of new rules/provisions reflecting the trends of the current (both technological and business) environment. To this aim, more important than the exact content of such rules will be the method for their effectiveness; i.e.,

---

[26] I.e. solutions independent of the particular nature of the specific technology used.

under the scope of the principles governing a democratic society, new, fast, flexible and "open" processes should be become effective either for the production or the application or the promotion of law.

The Commission encourages coordination of policies between Member States at many levels, including the sector of Internet management; in particular, this becomes effective by defining a proper framework for the organisation and the configuration of any corresponding activities. Taking into account the fact that the Internet provides significant benefits to users and access to a great range of digital sources, the creation of conditions for its secure usage and for combating technical illegal uses, is of major importance for any future policy. Simultaneously, as for Internet's content regulation the general principle will be the assurance of the requirement for the fulfilling of some basic EU policies aiming to promote, *inter-alia*, human dignity, cultural and linguistic diversity, pluralism, national and local sensitivities.

There is no doubt that the regulatory framework has a very significant role to play, in order to guarantee users' trust and confidence in the new innovative environment.

5.10 The Role of the Regulatory Provisions Regulatory Intervention vs. Self-Regulation and Co-Regulation

Overview of the current state

Taking into account the need for the continuous development and for the re-evaluation of the existing national and European legislations, it should be necessary to promote the appliance of a revised framework for the new applications; this will recognise any market uncertainties and the need for suitable investments -where necessary, and at least for a starting point-, while simultaneously it will consider the consumer protection and other targets for the public benefit.

Within such a reality, self-regulation (or co-regulation) could complete, for the aims of the wider global benefit, any existing regulatory initiative(s) or measure(s) and could contribute for the achievement of a "correct" equivalence between the development of open and competitive market conditions and the assurance of the appliance of the EU Treaty. An indicative example is the case of self-regulation for Internet content monitoring and management[27], via the development of modern tools for content filtering and rating systems provided by the industry sector, as well as the reinforced international co-operation for the assurance of a safe operational environment, for the deletion of any barriers and for the development of the competitiveness of the sector. Of significant importance is the role that should be performed by the private sector, especially for the protection of consumers' interests, via the forwarding and the acceptance of suitable codes of conduct. The introduction of proper systems for self-regulation will provide new potential; however, such systems should be based on and will be supported by both the guidelines and the rest of the provisions of the existing law.

It is evident that enterprises should be encouraged to deploy national co-operative activities and to promote mutual interaction with other interested parties, as self-regulation provides an opportunity for almost immediate adaptation to the accelerated technical progress and to markets of global scale.

The voluntary nature of self-regulation (with primary vision the completion of the existing regulation while respecting the multiple national attributes and sensitivities), implicates that acceptance and efficiency of any national framework for self-regulation (*including any attempt for definition, evaluation and applicability*) strongly depends on the extend of the active participation of any of the parties concerned (originating from the State, the users or the industry sector).

During the procedure for the definition of the basic rules for self-regulation, the principle guidelines should be the applicability of the fundamental context of the EU Law (including, *for example*, options for the protection of privacy, the free movement of goods and services, etc.) together with any intention of technical or business origin. In any case, the final target always remains the promotion of the Information Society. Furthermore, the creation of trust and security at global level may also ensure respect of principal human rights and coverage of various social and societal expectations.

In a fast moving environment, self-regulation has been advocated by industry as a strong tool, which is better adopted to answer

---

[27] See, for example, Council Resolution of 3 October 2000, on the organisation and management of the Internet, (OJ C293, 14.10.2000).

the dual challenge of rapidly increasing speed and scope; i.e. a tool to better deliver solutions in the fast-changing global economy. In any case, self-regulation may act as a flexible, efficient and cost-effective alternative to regulation in many areas. This implicates that for some specific cases and under exact criteria, there will be an adequate framework for the deletion of low, cumbersome, long-termed and bureaucratic procedures, to promote technical and economic efficiency of the Information Society applications. For the effectiveness of any relevant activity, of substantial importance will be any probable coordination between self-regulation initiatives at European level. This, once again implicates the need for "open" participation of all the players involved, simultaneously with the promotion and the use of more generalised codes of conduct, always aligned with the EU principles.

However, certain conditions must be met. Self-regulation is a complementary element to the current legislation; so it fully accepts the existing state as for both European and national legislation, and its aim is to contribute, *in a way*, to the fast applicability of some solutions, to skip over any potential or existing limitations for the promotion of the Information Society. Before any initiative, the European regulator should ensure compliance with the principles of equality, freedom, and should preserve the orientation to the democratic ideals to avoid any risks; this implicates the strong need for respect of rights, for transparency and for security of law. Market competition rules cannot be an adequate guarantee, if considered alone. The protection of healthy competition is of course a fundamental condition, but needs to be considered in parallel with other options for political, social and cultural pluralism.

The State would provide mechanisms to guarantee equal access to infrastructure and to information and measures for the promotion of multiple competitive offers to the markets. This may include, *inter-alia*, initiatives for the participation of all market players into the "chain" of the Internet industry. Self-regulation does not mean self-enforcement. It has to be in conformity with, and backed by law, while at the same time has to be enforceable, verifiable and auditable. Simultaneously it has to be effective, particularly across borders. In any case, self-regulation is not the "absolute" solution to all challenges; in particular, some nationally based self-regulation may occasionally add barriers to the free circulation of services. However, in most cases self-regulation provides a useful economy of legislation, to avoid cumbersome lawmaking. More specifically, when the related attempts reflect not only business interests, but also public interests, the effectiveness is greater.

Co-regulation implies taking self-regulation a step further, as a more co-operative approach. This combines the advantages of legislation - more especially its predictable and binding nature - with the more flexible approach under self-regulation. Co-regulation has already been used in various fields, more particularly: (i) the "New Approach"[28], where the essential requirements are laid down in a framework directive, leaving business and industry to decide for themselves how to meet their obligations and; (ii) the possibility, introduced by the Maastricht Treaty, of using agreements between the social partners (on their own initiative or after consultation by the Commission) as an alternative method of regulation in various fields (such as for example, for working conditions and access to work). Public and private partners have to share responsibilities through negotiated agreements, to address a number of challenges[29]. The first is to identify specific areas where such activities can fit, as probable alternatives while reaching the same target. Due to the global development of the Information Society applications, such activities may refer, *among others*, to the defence of fundamental public interests, taxation issues, security and encryption issues and many more. Competition policy is also a major section, in particular to guarantee a suitable level playing field. The development of mutual obligations and responsibilities for all parties could be a good starting point.

Another challenge might be to identify conditions where co-regulation will work. This once again imposes the necessity for mutual interaction between the public and the private operators, with mutual exchange of ideas, arguments and experiences, to deliver comparable results. However, for any specific (or even a more generalised) case, transparency, openness and consensus criteria should define any relevant activity, to achieve the expected targets. Such criteria are very important to enjoy the necessary confidence and can be probably defined on a case-by-case basis.

---

[28] See previous comment nr.5.

[29] See, for example, Commission Communication "*eEurope 2002: Creating a EU Framework for the exploitation of public sector information*", COM(2001) 607 final, 23.10.2001.

5.11 Conclusion

Technology and market development, existing and/or potential barriers and regulatory initiatives, as previously discussed, all point out a varying environment for which detailed policies have to be set out. Future decisions for further policy making should originate from exact regulatory approaches and common methods adopted to all relevant sectors. Due to the speed, the potential and the power of innovation affected by the convergence of modern technologies, regulators should avoid specific approaches towards further and/or detailed extension of some existing regulation originating from traditional activities (such as from traditional telecommunications services and traditional broadcasting services) to new applications/services; in particular when the latter are innovative ones, and there is no direct or full correlation to the former. The set of any of the relevant regulation will be adapted to well-defined criteria and rules, following the principle of proportionality among the different sectors.

The basic priority of any regulatory initiative will be the full coverage of users' needs, in terms of offers, wider choices, improvement of quality of services and lowering of prices, with a parallel consideration of targets of the public interest. Such an approach is fully compatible to the policies governing the development of the Information Society for the improvement of the living standards.

Regulatory Authorities should ensure applicability of a clear and transparent regulatory framework, where enterprises will be able to invest under "reasonable" terms and to participate to the global "digital era". Where self-regulation may coexist, there will be no obstacle for investment and for market activation. This does not implicate that the above framework will be static; however, for any evolutionary progress, certain criteria have to be met, preserving a degree of flexibility in a rapidly changed environment.

Public and regulatory authorities have to ensure conditions for equal access of citizens and inclusion to the digital reality. While the latest general trends is towards creating "lighter" regulation (i.e. regulation with more flexibility and, proportionally, with less obligations to the market players), the increasing and global competition raises the necessity for effective legislation and for independent National Regulatory Authorities, able to supervise the full sector. In fact, any regulatory initiative (including self-regulation or co-regulation activities) will be a useful tool, able to contribute to the fulfilment of the social, political, financial, commercial and other EU expectations. However, any relevant initiative should take into account both the existing and the projected state of the market, by considering a variety of factors.

The global challenges, reinforced by the technical convergence, give to the market itself a very special perspective; i.e. market players have to interact, to exchange ideas and to co-operate, in order to ensure either equilibrium of the expected regulation or justification of conditions for healthy and transparent competition. Priority should be given to the promotion of effective converging measures, instead of extending existing regulation. Until recently, regulation and self-regulation were often seen as diametrically opposed. Governments and industry used to defend their "traditional" favourite instruments. However, strong pressures from the digital economy have led to a more inclusive approach, where integration takes place on the basis of mutual interest. To this aim, self-regulation has a key role to play and has been advocated by industry as a powerful tool to better deliver solutions in a fast-changing global economy. Within such a context, co-regulation implies taking self-regulation a step further; i.e. it implies sharing of responsibilities through negotiated agreements between public and private partners. Co-regulation empowers self-regulation by placing it in a wider clear framework, to mutually reinforce each other.

The key challenge for co-regulation is to define, maintain and preserve policy goals, while allowing for flexibility in the drawing up and the implementation of these policy goals. For any activity, the mutual cooperation of the involved parties is more than necessary, while different forms of partnerships can further contribute to the promotion of the common EU policies.

Internet Security: Now and in the Future

6.1 Introduction

This chapter discusses common Internet security technologies and blended Internet security methods with references to other areas where biometrics technologies have been adopted. For centuries, security was synonymous with secrecy. The shared secret between two parties conducting business was a worldwide approach. But secret passwords require a great deal of trust between parties sharing the secret. *Can we always trust the administrator or other users of the Internet network service provider that we access?*

Most computer break-ins today are due to compromise by system users or hackers who use legitimate accounts to gain access to general security. Determining the identity of a person is becoming critical in our vastly connected information society. As a large number of biometrics-based identification systems are being deployed for many civilian and forensic applications, biometrics and its application have evoked considerable interest. Accenture [1], predicts that the "Internet economy will top US $1 trillion by the end of 2002." No one can afford to ignore the presence of the Internet economy or its future potential growth. Analysts suggest that there is no way of making the Internet "100 percent safe," therefore, organisations and government are forced to implement security policies, technological software and regulations in order to control unauthorised intrusion into corporate networks [2].

Corporate data are at risk when they are exposed to the Internet. Current technologies provide a number of ways to secure data transmission and storage, but other approaches to Internet security focus on protecting the contents of electronic transmissions and verification of individual users. Secure electronic transmissions are an important condition for conducting business on the Internet.

Biometrics technology that uses the human beings' physical or behavioural traits for identification purposes will play an important role in the near future of desktop computing, mobile phones, and, in particular, access to institutional computers and sensitive data via the Internet.

Because the Internet uses Simple transfer protocol (SMTP) anyone can obtain messages & the contents included, with a word processing program.

6.2 Improving Security to Control Physical Access

Security is a major concern for Internet users and system administrators. Whether to protect confidential data and information in individual files, lock a computer system to unauthorised users, control access to an intranet or an extranet, or conduct business on the Internet, one needs to determine an appropriate level of security and the effective means to achieve the objectives. The threat to Internet security is one of the main barriers to electronic transaction via the Internet medium. With the current popularity and the potential profits of electronic business, many executives face a conflict situation. That is, connecting to the Internet and expanding their business would lead to risks and threats of intrusion. On the other hand, remaining disconnected from the Internet would sacrifice their customer contact and services to their competitors.

The Internet uses simple mail transfer protocol (SMTP) to transmit electronic mail and most business transactions. These transmissions have as much privacy as a postcard and travel over insecure, untrusted lines. Anyone anywhere along the transmission path can obtain access to a message and read the contents with a simple text viewer or word processing program. Because the transmission lines are insecure, it is easy to forge e-mail or use another person's name. Theft of identity is becoming the nation's leading incidence of fraud. A person can even claim that someone else sent a message, for example, to cancel an order or avoid paying an invoice.

Organisations in both the public and the private sectors are aware of the needs of Internet security. It is interesting to know how

Public & private organisations realise the absolute requirements of Internet Security

both sectors take action to protect their Internet data and corporate systems. The best way to keep an intruder from entering the network is to provide a security wall between the intruder and the corporate network. Since the intruders enter the network through a software program, such as a virus or worm etc., or a direct connection, firewalls, data encryption, and user authentication can restrain a hacker to some extent. *One way of improving security*

The first objective to improving security is to control physical access by limiting it to authorised individuals. The principle is that the fewer people who can get physical and administrative access to sensitive files or to server systems, the greater the security will be. Most applications rely on passwords, personal identification numbers, and keys to access restricted information or confidential files. Passwords, cards, personal identification numbers and keys can be forgotten, stolen, forged, lost or given away. Moreover, these devices serve primarily to identify the person. They cannot verify or authenticate that the person really is who he or she claims to be.

The information age is quickly revolutionising the way transactions are completed. Everyday actions are increasingly being handled electronically, instead of with pencil and paper or face to face. This growth in electronic transactions has resulted in a greater demand for fast and accurate user identification and authentication. Biometric technology is a way to achieve fast, user-friendly authentication with a high level of accuracy.

— look up.

6.3   Current Developments in Internet Security

Every industry has its own particular needs and requires certain safeguards to protect its data from damage. The public and private sectors have their own strengths and weaknesses on Internet security. Each industry requires certain safeguards to protect its data while in transit. Developing a plan that has proportionately more strength than weakness is always the goal. However, the Internet is an untamed frontier that is still young and growing. It may take some time to develop stronger methods for data security.

Protecting an organisation from the perils of the Internet is similar to the job of a security guard working during the night shift: As long as he stays awake and keeps his eyes open, the chances are that

169

nothing will happen. While companies arm themselves with the latest IDS and virus software, there is still a chance that someone from the outside can get in and wreak havoc on the company's system. Software and hardware configurations keep most of the intruders at bay, but being able to recognise abnormal activity when it occurs seems to be the best method. This requires a well trained IT staff to constantly monitor the network for deviants, using the system software to set up audits in all the right places. As technology continues to evolve and software and hardware improvements are implemented, there may come a time when hackers not only will be forced to stay outside the company walls, but also will be exposed by law enforcement during the process.

The future of Internet security, therefore, resides in human intervention and innovation. Implementing hardware and software solutions, as well as using human intervention to continually monitor the network, are two of the best ways to keep abreast of attacks from the outside.

One of the latest technologies in the security market, which was introduced at the NetWorld + Interop trade show in Atlanta, is a technology called adaptive security. This development is a result of Internet Security Systems' (ISS) formation of the Adaptive Network Security Alliance (ANSA) around an application program interface for its real secure intrusion detection system [3]. The technology requires the enlistment of major infrastructure vendors, such as 3Com, Lucent, Compaq, Entrust and Checkpoint, to enable their products to talk with ISS's intrusion detection monitors. By communicating between ISS's monitor and the vendor's products, firewalls and switches could be reconfigured in response to perceived break-ins, thereby diminishing the lag time between detection and prevention and ultimately, making the network virtually impossible to penetrate.

In addition, SSL, the standard for secure Internet transmissions used by credit card companies, may get a face-lift in the near future. To improve the security between themselves and their customers, the credit card companies have been developing another standard called the secure electronic transaction (SET) standard, which may have an effect on the security of Internet transaction. SET focuses on confidentiality and authentication. SET-compliant software will not only make sure that thieves cannot steal a credit card number, but also keep a merchant from seeing the number while still providing assurances that the card is valid. The transmission will pass through the merchant's hands directly to the credit card user, which will then decrypt it and credit the merchant's account [4].

The possibility of the back-end authentication process (in a networked situation) being compromised by the passing of illegal data may represent a point of vulnerability. The authentication engine and its associated interface could be fooled. It is necessary to suggest a measure of risk to the biometrics system in use, especially when the authentication engine may not be able to verify that it is receiving a bona fide live transaction data (and not a data stream from another source). Even a highly accurate biometrics system can reject authorised users, fail to identify known users, identify users incorrectly, or allow unauthorised person to verify as known users. In addition, if a third-party network is utilised as part of the overall biometrics system – for example using the Internet to connect remotely to corporate networks – the end-to-end connection between host controller and back-end application server should be carefully considered.

However, in most cases, biometrics system cannot determine if an individual has established a fraudulent identity, or is posing as another individual during biometrics enrolment process. An individual with a fake passport may be able to use the passport as the basis of enrolment in a biometrics system. The system can only verify that the individual is who he or she claimed to be during enrolment, unless a large-scale identification system is built in which all users are matched against all other users to find duplicates or individual attempts to enrol more than once.

6.4 Blended Internet Security Methods

The past decade has witnessed dramatic changes in business processes. The number of organisations that store and access confidential and business-critical data in digital form on computer networks or over the Internet has increased dramatically. The importance of Internet security will therefore become an important aspect as the threat-level of electronic crime increases. Although the global community has gained numerous benefits from using new computing technologies, these technologies have at the same time made the wired community more vulnerable to breaches in electronic information transfer security.

Biometrics has been used for years in high-security government and military applications, but the technology is now becoming affordable for use as a network authentication method and general security feature. It is tempting to think of biometrics as being sci-fi futuristic technology that we should in the near future use together with solar-powered cars, food pills, and other fiendish devices. There are many references to individuals being formally identified via unique physiological parameters such as scars, measured physical criteria or a combination of features such as complexion, eye colour, height, etc.

Automated biometrics has been in existence for more than 30 years now. As we know, matching fingerprints against criminal records is important for the law enforcers to find the criminal. But the manual process of matching is very tedious and time-consuming. In 1960s, the Federal Bureau of Investigation (FBI) in U.S. began to automatically check finger images and by 1970s a good number of automatic finger-scanning systems had been installed. Among these systems, Identimat was the first commercial one. The system measured the shape of the hand and looked particularly at finger length [5]. Its use pioneered the application of hand geometry and set path for biometric technologies as a whole.

Internet security methods can work together within a network in various ways. Figure 5 below illustrates how common Internet security technologies such as a firewall or remote access service (RAS) server with biometrics user authentication can be used to protect against data intrusion from the outside and within. If a user tries to access this server with combined biometrics and is not authorised to do so, the IDS will alert information technology (IT) staff of that entry, even though the user may or may not have the right biometrics user authentication. Since the IDS uses both static and dynamic monitoring systems to monitor direct attacks and abnormal network accesses, the server is dually protected from potential harm.

The graph
Using the Internet with combined biometrics allows for detection of unauthorised uses, by alerting IT staff.

172

Figure 5: Combining Common Internet Security Technologies with Biometrics

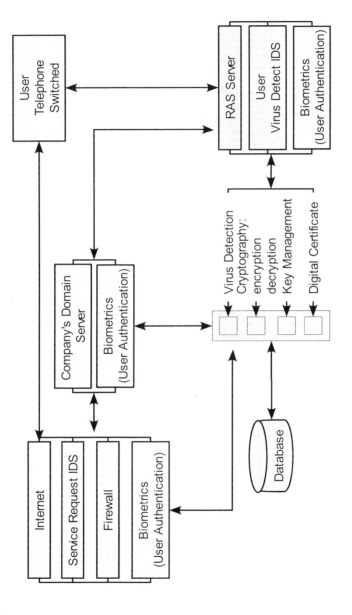

Data encryption is also used throughout the network. Users calling in from a switched telephone network to a RAS server on a Windows NT network can use data encryption via point-to-point tunnelling protocol (PPTP) to exchange data from their laptop or home computer to the Internet through the corporate network and vice versa. When a user connects to the network through a RAS server, the user is given the same access right as any other user in the company. The user can connect to the RAS server and send encrypted data to another computer or server using PPTP. The RAS server also has its own safeguards, such as user call-back to a specific phone number to establish a connection and user authentication, encrypted passwords and user permissions.

Data encryption can be implemented between a corporate server and a vendor or supplier through an extranet. If data security is imperative on an extranet, both parties could use encryption to ensure privacy and data protection. By incorporating a virtual private network (VPN) on an extranet, both a company and its supplier can ensure maximum data protection on the Internet.

In addition to extranets and VPN, digital certificates and key management are two other alternatives for data security. If a company has an enterprise network that spans a large geographical area, corporate officials could use this technology to protect sensitive data from unauthorised access. For example, if the human resources and finance departments need to share sensitive data, they could communicate through the corporate intranet and use key management to protect the data and digital certificates to verify the accuracy of transmission.

Even though the VPNs and extranets provide some type of security, key management and digital certificates are simply two more locks and keys that could be set in place for peace of mind. Setting up a secured network is a daunting task. It requires careful thought, adequate planning and the perspectives and recommendations of a team of IT staff. The Internet service provider network should be configured so that it is scalable and flexible to handle additional hardware and software as the network grows with combined Internet security technologies and biometrics.

Indeed, much attention has been paid to biometrics in recent months as a means to increase security for public places and businesses. Biometrics technology is superior to other identification solutions because it verifies a person's identity based on a unique physical

174

attribute rather than some paper or plastic ID card, and as such, the number of biometric implementations is on the rise. Public awareness and acceptance of biometrics is increasing steadily as well. People realise the improved safety this technology offers us collectively as a society.

The Newham Borough Council is a case in point where biometric technology has been adopted to combat the frequent street crimes within the Borough. The Newham Borough Council in east London uses a facial recognition system in a closed-circuit television (CCTV) control-room application as part of an anti-crime initiative. FaceIt, from the US firm Visionics, is part of a CCTV-based system called Mandrake. The Mandrake system uses the FaceIt software in conjunction with other control-room software and hardware to automatically scan the faces of people passing 144 CCTV cameras located around Newham. The system's objective is to reduce crime in Newham by searching for matches in a video library of known criminals stored in a local police database.

Biometrics provides greater protection of our personal data and financial assets, which more essential than ever before. Biometrics can better safeguard our most critical data that could cause us the most harm if accessed by the wrong person. Some of the biggest potential applications include the use of biometrics for access to Automated Teller Machines (ATM) or for use with credit or debit cards and as a general use for combating credit card fraud. Many types of financial transactions are also potential applications e.g., banking by phone, banking by Internet, and buying and selling securities by telephone or by Internet.

In the US, several states have saved significant amounts of money by implementing biometric verification procedures. Not surprisingly, the numbers of benefits claims has dropped dramatically in the process, validating the systems as an effective deterrent against multiple claims.

With as little as a home address, driver's license number or bank account number, criminals can use the Internet to find out all kinds of personal information about an individual. In some US prisons, visitors to inmates are subject to verification procedures in order that identities are not swapped during the visit. Criminals can obtain the necessary data to get new credit cards issued in your name, print fake checks in your name, obtain bank loans in your name, and perpetrate other creative scams in your name to profit at your expense. By the time you find out what has happened, serious damage can be done. Victims of identity theft often spend years and thousands of dollars clearing their names and credit reports.

Implementing payment-processing systems that utilise biometrics with private account management can easily prevent credit card crime. Biometrics can be incorporated at the point of sale, thereby enabling consumers to enrol their payment options e.g., checking, credit, debit, loyalty, etc., into a secure electronic account that is protected by, and accessed with, a unique physical attribute such as a fingerprint. Cash, cards or cheques are not needed to make purchases, so there is no need to carry them in a purse or wallet. Not carrying a purse or wallet eliminates the chances of it being stolen or lost while shopping.

Biometric transaction-processing systems allow consumers to manage point-of-sale payment easily and securely. This solution is particularly well suited for personal check use. Biometrics can also offer increased protection for check-cashing services, whether personal or payroll. By requiring biometric identity verification before allowing a check to be cashed, the possibility of it being presented by anyone other than the intended payee is eliminated.

Biometrics technologies, has been gaining recognition as a security solution that can improve the collective safety of society, and it is undoubtedly useful in this manner. Since the September 11 terrorist attack on US, many questions have been raised concerning airport security. Although biometrics technology alone could not have prevented the September 11 attacks from happening, biometrics can be implemented as one component of a security system. A biometrics verification and identification can ensure that a person is who he or she claims to be, or can identify a person from a database of trusted or suspect individuals. If the identity of a traveller or employee is in question, biometrics can be a highly effective solution. An individual using a forged or stolen badge or ID card, if required to verify biometrically before entering a secure area, would likely be detected if his or her biometric does not matched the biometric on file. An individual claiming a fraudulent ID can be identified from a database of known criminals and linked to biometric identification systems, which may prevent him or her from boarding an airplane.

The UK's Barclays Bank has been using finger-scan technology for employee access to buildings since 1996 and is also currently involved in a pilot program for PC logins to the corporate networks. In 1998, Nationwide Building Society became the first organisation in the world to trial iris recognition technology supplied by ATM manufacturer NCR. 91 percent of their customers said they would choose iris identification over PINs or signatures in the future [6, 7].

6.5 Discussion

Government agencies, businesses and consumers are increasingly recognising the limitations of passwords and PIN numbers as computer hacking, identify theft and other forms of cyber crime become more prevalent. Biometrics devices offer a higher level of security because they verify physiological or behavioural characteristics that are unique to each individual and are difficult to forge. Biometrics devices also relieve security personnel, network managers and customer service representatives of the tedious and often intrusive tasks of identity verification and password/PIN administration.

Personal identification numbers were one of the first identifiers to offer automated recognition. However, it should be understood that this means recognition of the PIN, not necessarily recognition of the person who has provided it. The same applies with cards and other tokens. We may easily recognise the token, but it could be presented by anybody. Using the two together provides a slightly higher confidence level, but this is still easily compromised if one is determined to do so.

A biometric, however, cannot be easily transferred between individuals and represents a unique identifier as compared with the traditional PIN. In practice this means that verifying an individual's identity can become both more efficient and considerably more accurate as biometric devices are not easily fooled. In the context of travel and tourism, for example, one immediately thinks of immigration control, boarding gate identity verification and other security related functions. Everyday questions such as, *"should this person be given access to a secure system?" "Does this person have authorisation to perform a given transaction?"* and *"Is this person a citizen of our country?"* are asked millions of times.

All these questions deal with how to correctly identify human beings. Currently there are two popular ways of solving such security problems. One is related to something most of us have, such as credit cards, physical keys, etc., and the other depends on something that we are familiar with, such as a password or PIN. Both methods give the authority to some media, such as password or keys, other than end users. If a user gets the password or other media, he will get the authority; otherwise he loses the authority. Under such a security schema, people have to keep various cards and remember tens of passwords.

Losing a card or forgetting password may bring users into great deal of trouble. In the meanwhile, banks, telecommunication companies and other government set-ups are suffering from losing millions of pounds per year due to the breaches of current card or password based security systems. In order to solve this problem, researchers are trying various ways of solving these problems and biometrics approach is most promising.

Biometrics is a technology that uses human beings unique physical or behavioural features to identify or verify persons. It relies on "something that you are" to make a personal identification and therefore can inherently differentiate between authorised person and a fraudulent impostor. Because one's unique characteristics cannot be stolen, forgotten, duplicated, shared or observed, biometrics-based security system is nearly impossible to fraud. This does not mean that biometrics is a universal remedy for all our personal identification related issues, but they do represent an interesting new tool in our technology tool box, which we might usefully consider as we march forward into the new millennium.

Recognition based on retina, iris, voice evolved during 1970s, while signature and facial verification are relatively new. In the nineteenth century, there was a peak of interest as researchers into criminology attempted to relate physical features and characteristics with criminal tendencies. With this background, it is hardly surprising that for many years a fascination with the possibility of using electronics and the power of microprocessors to automate identity verification had occupied the minds of individuals and organisations both in the military and commercial sectors. The role of biometrics in law enforcement has grown rapidly since the 1960s and automated fingerprint identification (AFIS) is used by a significant number of police throughout the world. A widespread commercial adoption of biometrics is unlikely to take place until there are universal standards in place. Such standards should, in theory, make biometric technology consistent, interoperable and interchangeable. This will in turn encourage more end users to experiment with the biometric technology.

It is equally important to mention that there is no perceived simple manner in which to integrate biometric authentication mechanisms into existing applications. However, the early implementers of biometric technology have found themselves limited to single application implementations based on single vendor product offerings. This limits the use of such technology in any practical sense.

Consumers in the Internet marketplace want to control what personal information is disclosed about them, to whom, and how that information will be used and further distributed. The state of the art technology has been addressed and pointed out the imminent integration of business self-regulation and the consumer's ability to enhance individual privacy protection through the use of technology. We need emerging technologies to protect privacy on the Internet. Depending on the type of business and the value of the data, a company has the choice of using virtual private networks, digital certificates, data encryption, and network operating systems to protect their data while in transit, ensure the identity of a user, and mask the data from unauthorised eyes.

However, the future is not all rosy. There remains much that needs to be done in order to make the Internet a widely acceptable marketplace for the exchange of goods and services between merchants and consumers. Technology continues to become more complex; the safeguards used today may be severely out of date tomorrow.

Biometric will be most effective when used in tandem with other security measures. Strong encryption is not the answer to every security issue. Buggy software, human error and greed and poor server administration provide opportunities for unscrupulous hackers. The increasing number of private communications over the Web, particularly business transactions, will require a higher level of security. If a problem occurs with a business transaction or a Web company is accused of bad business practices, it may become very difficult to establish liability. *Who should be held accountable – the business, the bank, or the trust intermediary?* The authentication may become an important condition of conducting business electronically.

Many questions concerning biometrics remain unanswered: *"Will it produce an underworld of cyber criminals who pose a threat to the very structure of the society?" "To what extent can companies trust their employees with sensitive employees coded biometrics information?"* Indeed, companies cannot ignore the problems of Internet security as this would result in the loss of competitive advantage in the market place. What the future holds for Internet security technology such as biometrics cannot be predicted to the rate technology is advancing.

The ethical issues surrounding biometrics technologies are of grave concern. The right to privacy is one of our most cherished freedoms. As society grows more complex and people become more interconnected in every way, we must work even harder to respect the privacy, dignity and autonomy of each individual. We must develop new protection for privacy in the face of new technological reality [8].

This issue of privacy is central to biometrics. Critics complain that the use of biometrics poses a substantial risk to privacy rights. Evaluating this argument requires a proper understanding of what privacy rights entails. But if biometrics are the way forward in making sure that all transactions are fully secure then the questions to ask are: *"How much will it cost to implement such security solution(s)?"*, *"Who should be trust with genetics information?"*, and *"How long will it take the expert hacker to decrypt such human genetic codes?"* These are some of the concerns of businesses and online shoppers.

Indeed, the human race has not only brought its business to cyberspace, it has brought its exploration of the psyche there, too. In the digital world, just as everywhere else, humanity has encountered its dark side. Information Age business, government, and culture have led to Information Age crime, Information Age war and even Information Age terror [2, 9, 10].

6.6 Conclusion

It is a well-established fact that the traditional security measures such as password and identification cards cannot satisfy every security requirement. Various physiological and behavioural biometrics for the authentication of individuals have broader applications such as the control of access to personal computers, private files and information repositories, building access control, and many others. Although biometrics is still relatively expensive and immature, integrated multiple biometrics features such as fingerprints, palm prints, facial features and voice patterns to authenticate a person's identity and verify his or her eligibility to access the Internet are in the development stage. The biometrics devices will continue to improve, becoming even more accurate and reliable as Internet technology evolves.

As biometrics technology becomes more acceptable, the proliferation of applications should multiply into many phases of our daily activities. The growing interest in combining common Internet security technologies with biometrics will increase the growth and popularity of blended Internet security methods in the future. Nevertheless the ethical issues surrounding biometrics technologies must be weighed against any potential benefits.

References

1   Accenture (2001) 'Internet economy will top $1 trillion by end of 2001', *Financial Times,* 19 March.

2   Shoniregun, C.A., (2002) 'Are existing Internet security measures guaranteed to protect user identity in the financial services industry?', *Int. J. Services Technology and Management,* Vol. 4, No. 2, 2003, pp.194-216.

3   Eschelbeck, G., (2000), "Active Security: A proactive approach for computer security systems", *Network and Computer Application,* 23, pp. 109-130.

4   *PC Magazine* (1999), "The future of Internet security", March.

5   Zhang, D.D., (2000) 'Automated Biometrics Technology and Systems', Kluwer Academic.

6   Desmarais, N. (2000) 'Body language, security and E-commerce', *Library Hi Tech,* Vol. 18, No. 1, pp.6174.

7   White, M. (2001) 'Networking in a networked economy', *Finance on Windows,* Summer pp.8283.

8   Clinton W.J., (1997), Commencement Address at Morgan State University, 18 May.

9   Liu, *et al.* (2001) E-Commerce Agents, Marketplace Solutions, Security Issues, and Supply and Demand, Springer.

10   Timmers, P. (2000) Electronic Commerce (Strategies and Models for Business-to-Business Trading), John Wiley.

Bibliography

Oppliger R. (2002) Internet and Intranet Security, Second edition, Artech House Publishers.

Proctor P.E. (2002) The Practical Intrusion Handbook, Prentice Hall.

Appendix 1:

Producers and Virtual Retail Outlets Dynamic Business Model on Implementation of eC

To achieve the success in implementing this model, it is necessary to iterate between the phases and levels. This model consists of two phases, and within each phase are two other detailed levels:

Figure 6: Dynamic Business Model, Phase 1

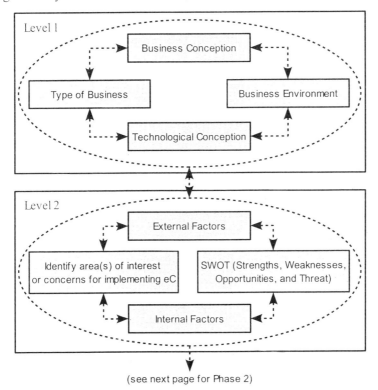

(see next page for Phase 2)

Phase 1 looks at the steps in which Producers and Virtual Retail Outlets small business enterprise can analyse their E-business needs

Type of Business
- Physical item(s) provider
- Service(s) provider
- other businesses

Business and Technological conception
The business ideas or other ideas from the existing marketplace:
- Comparing different business Web sites
- Compatibility technology in

Business Environment
- Feasibility study
- Government policy towards businesses
- Economics
- Culture
- Competitive Analysis (Porter's five forces)

Identify area(s) of interest or concerns for implementing eC
- How can the business take advantages of Internet – eC
- Will the business offer its customers something distinctive or a lower cost than its competitors will
- Staff
- Security

SWOT
- Strengths/Weaknesses (Internal Factors):
  The current internal competencies and ability to support eC
- Opportunities/Threat (External factors):
  The current market and role of eC in the business sector

To achieve the success in implementing this model, it is necessary to iterate between phases and levels.

Figure 7: Dynamic Business Model, Phase 2

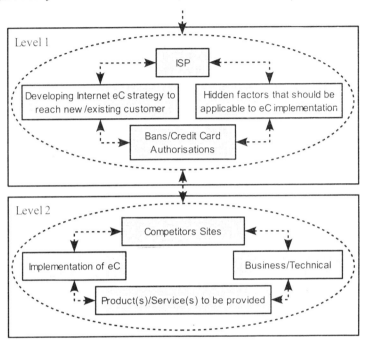

Phase 2 looks at the hidden factors which needs to be considered in when developing eC /or E-business strategies

Developing eC Strategy

- How new activities will be performing as a result of the Internet?

- How can the Internet help to perform existing activities (business operations)?

- What does the Internet eC do to the strategy, business operation, staff and the customers?

Hidden Factors (Costing, Human Resources, Marketing and Sales)

- Scope (Product(s) /or Service(s) range)

185

- Customer value
- Finance (Where is the capital or loan going to come from)
- Possible revenue that might be able to generate from the eC site
- Link to suppliers database and delivery
- Back office and supplies
- Staff / People (training, and recruitment)
- Culture
- Does the business have sustainable competitive advantages?
- Is the business product(s) or service(s) a niche market type?
- Internet catalogue and customer care
- Connected activities (ISP and Bank / Credit Cards charges)

Implementation of eC and Business / Technical elements

- Complete coverage of a market niche
- Can the ISP provide a developer to build the business site or recommend a developer
- Consult a Web design developer and the costing
- Business owner / staff dedication
- Can business get some help from the government
- Can business have Internet eC built now and pay later by instalment
- The anticipated system configuration will involve a customised market survey
- System integration (hardware and software to meet necessary business requirements)

Appendix 2:

SWOT of Cybermediation from Producers and Virtual Retail Outlets (VRO) Businesses Perspective

Most businesses are likely to select just few key factors and issues relevant to them, and will then analyse them systematically in terms of SWOT (Strengths, Weaknesses, Opportunities and Threats). An example of the points that might arise in such an analysis is given in this appendix, highlighted numbers of the issues faced by the 30 producers and virtual retail outlets were interviewed, currently using eC as part of or their day-to-day business operations. The SWOT analysis can be used as a framework by both bricks and mortar, and a purely e-business type in the Phase 1: Level 1, of our proposed, dynamic business model (see Appendix 1).

Factor / Issues discussed at the structure interviewed	Strengths	30 Producers &VRO's responses (n=30)	
		Yes	No
❑ Cybermediation contribution business	• Greater organisational efficiency through the use of access database and online shopping cart, tighter customer retention due to online feedback and easy communication methods.	29	1
	• The businesses are not E-start businesses, therefore if the solution should fail it would not mean failure for the business to serve the existing customers.	20	10
❑ Business transactions	• Quicker transactions due to online shopping catalogue	28	2
❑ Customer base	• Lower cost of products to clients due to businesses streamlining and higher expected turnover	26	4
❑ Market share	• Market competitiveness due to Web presence and wider customer base	29	1
❑ Product range/Attractivenes	• Method of advertising the business products/services	30	0

Factor / Issues discussed at the structure interviewed	Weaknesses	30 Producers & VRO's responses (n=30)	
		Yes	Yes
☐ Advertising campaign	• To date there is no clear marketing strategy or advertising campaign within the business apart from the web site	26	4
☐ Connectivity and language barriers	• Inability to connect to foreign databases slow down the implementation of online sales and bookings	22	8
☐ Market share	• Less secure in some market	27	3
☐ Product range/ attractiveness	• Other web sites can be considered to be much attractive and offer greater functionality	30	0
☐ Financial position	• Lack of investment means Search engines are unlikely to put the web sites at the top of the so-called list	30	0
☐ Hidden factors in eC Implementation	• Lack of dynamic business model on how to implementation of eC with existing legacy systems	30	0

Factor / Issues discussed at the structure interviewed	Opportunities	30 Producers & VRO's responses (n=30)	
		Yes	Yes
☐ Customer base	• Sustain growth through product range and staff efficiency	25	5
☐ eC contribution to business	• Implementation of the web site offers greater streamlining of business and further organisation and efficiency within the business due to the integrated technology database	22	8
☐ Product range / Attractiveness	• Improve bulk purchase	30	0
☐ Market share	• The business operates in a niche market where the competition offered is far less	15	15
☐ Financial position	• Trading in a global market business place, help to strengthen position in the markets	16	14
☐ Financial position	• Focus on improving reductions in cost while maintaining quality	25	5

Factor / Issues discussed at the structure interviewed	Threats	30 Producers & VRO's responses (n=30)	
		Yes	Yes
❑ Customer base	• Competitors activity. The most apparent threat to the small business is other businesses offering the same product or services using eC solutions	30	0
❑ Financial position	• Other eC small businesses that are prepared to invest heavily in their web site technology, these businesses are more likely to be frequent visits by E-clients	17	13
❑ Internet Service Provider	• The web sites are dependent upon the web host functioning as required, if the web host fails for some reason then so dose the web site	30	0
❑ Market share	• Weak business operations could take years to reach profit	30	0
❑ Product range / attractiveness	• Failure to recognise what product the customer wants	30	0
	• Imposition of VAT on products /or services on the Internet	15	15
	• Price-cutting by main competitors	29	1
❑ Security measures	• The lack of confidence from E-clients with regard to security may be a real problem for the development and use of many small business sites	30	0
❑ Web site(s)	• Increasing costs of maintaining the site(s) e.g. security measures against hackers	28	2

Index of Companies Referenced

191

Index of Keywords

193

195

International Journal for Infonomics

ISSN 1742-4720 (online) ISSN 1742-4712 (print)

Call for Papers

Theme

Infonomics is an interdisciplinary science studying evolution of and processes within the information society. By its nature, infonomics is the intelligent management of information.

Topics of Interest

The International Journal for Infonomics will organise the first issue to be published in March-April 2004. We invite original and high quality submissions addressing all aspects of infonomics and e-society. The IJI encourages both technical and non-technical contributions, which comply with the mission and fall into, but not limited by, the following list of topics:

- e-Society
- e-Government
- e-Commerce and Management
- e-Business Ethics
- e-Security and e-Risk,
- e-Tailing and e-Procurement
- e-Art
- e-Education
- e-Learning

- Intellectual Property Rights in Digital Society
- Regulating Distortions and Cyber Frauds
- Secured Electronic Transactions
- Advances in Encryption
- New Enabling Technologies
- Globalisation and Developmental IT

- Knowledge Economy
- Enterprise Resource Models
- Electronic Customer Relationship Management (e-CRM)
- Implications of Digital Convergence
- Geographic Information Systems
- Social Informatics
- Intelligent Data Management
- Intelligent Organisations
- Knowledge Networks and Intelligent Agents
- e-Intelligence

For further details, please, visit the IJI website at www.infonomics.org.uk.